For the Liberation of Brazil

Carlos Marighela was an orthodox and leading Communist
in São Paulo until 1967, when he attended the conference
of the Organization for Latin American Solidarity (OLAS)
against his party's wishes. In 1968 he and Mario Alves set
up their own pro-Cuban Revolutionary Communist Party of
Brazil. In the same year he launched Action for National
Liberation (ALN), a series of armed uprisings against the
forces of fascist repression in Brazil. In his letters and
pamphlets Marighela emphasized the importance of adapting
the strategy of the *foco*, pioneered by Guevara and Debray in
the countryside, for use in the towns. By 1969 revolutionary
bandits had taken £400,000 from the banks of Rio and
São Paulo alone, and had gained widespread support from
many sections of the population. After the kidnapping
of the United States ambassador had succeeded in securing
the release of fifteen rebel prisoners, the military junta
resorted to terror and torture in double measure. On
4 November 1969 Marighela was shot dead by police.

Carlos Marighela

For the Liberation
of Brazil

*Translated by John Butt
and Rosemary Sheed*

*With an Introduction by
Richard Gott*

 Penguin Books

Penguin Books Ltd, Harmondsworth,
Middlesex, England
Penguin Books Inc., 7110 Ambassador Road,
Baltimore, Maryland 21207, U.S.A.
Penguin Books Australia Ltd, Ringwood,
Victoria, Australia

Published in Pelican Books 1971
Translation copyright © John Butt and Rosemary Sheed, 1971
Introduction copyright © Richard Gott, 1971

Made and printed in Great Britain by
Cox & Wyman Ltd, London, Reading and Fakenham
Set in Intertype Lectura

Contents

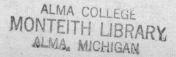

Introduction

Early in 1970 some parts of this book appeared in France* and in the middle of March in that year the *Journal Officiel* announced that the distribution and sale of the book would be forbidden throughout French territory. This action reflects more on the conservative nature of the present French régime than on the inherently subversive nature of the book, nevertheless it is interesting to find that the printed word is still considered to have such an explosive quality. More fascinating is the fact that a book about revolution in a distant Latin American country – although one of the largest and potentially one of the most important in the world – can be thought by the authorities in an advanced European country to be frighteningly relevant to their own crisis.

For the relevance is not always immediately apparent. What message can the guerrilla fighters of Latin America, whether rural or urban, bring to revolutionaries in the advanced industrialized world, with its vastly more sophisticated political structure? True, there is the inspiration to be gained from their actions and example: Che Guevara is an almost unique figure in world history, a man who helped lead a successful revolution and then threw everything up to start again at the bottom of the ladder; Camilo Torres, too, was a rare soul: a priest and a sociologist, he abandoned the Church and the university to fight against the system of which they formed an integral part.

* *Carlos Marighela: Pour la Libération du Brésil*, presented by Conrad Detrez, Éditions du Seuil, 1970. The present edition contains much material not included in the French text.

Less well known, but equally interesting, is Carlos Marighela. A stalwart of the orthodox Communist Party, he rebelled in his late fifties against the bureaucratization of the Party which he had helped to build up, and he tried to create in Brazil a genuinely revolutionary movement.

But though these men may inspire, they do not at first sight provide a key to action, except perhaps for unlikely groups who believe that guerrilla action in the Pennines or the Vosges is the way forward. The reason why they are important is that they recognized the need to break with old revolutionary ideas and analyses.

They are part of a new movement of ideas that was given immense impetus in the mid sixties by the Cultural Revolution in China and by the propagation of the Maoist slogan, 'It is right to rebel'. It gained strength during the Bolivian guerrilla campaign of 1967, with its attendant publicity for the seemingly heretical ideas of Guevara and Régis Debray. And it achieved its highest pinnacle of success during the French revolution of May 1968, which indicated that the ideas were valid, if premature.

They had been neatly encapsulated in Debray's *Revolution in the Revolution?*, which by chance was published just a few months before its author was captured and accused by the Bolivian army of leading a guerrilla movement. The fact that Debray was French – and that President de Gaulle had appealed to his captors for clemency – gave his ideas more resonance in France than almost anywhere else, perhaps, more even than in Latin America. And the essence of Debray's message – that the hegemony of the old orthodox Communist Party had to be swept away – was powerful medicine in a country like France where the Communist Party, as in Italy, had dominated and overshadowed all other sections of the Left for decades.

In England and the United States, which almost entirely lack a Marxist tradition in intellectual life, the impact has been less marked. But even in those two stolidly pragmatic countries, the growth of an extra-parliamentary opposition, tired of the stale orthodoxy which demanded allegiance to a Labour or Democratic party, owes something to a movement which erected heresy into a new orthodoxy.

The importance in Latin America of Guevara and Debray was that they allowed the Left to escape from the straitjacket of orthodox thinking in which it had been tightly laced for many years. Marighela is important because he began to build on the foundations of this new tradition. Looking back over the past ten years, one can see that the Cuban revolution of 1959 did have a temporary effect in persuading people, deeply influenced by geographic fatalism, that revolution in the continent was really possible, in spite of the proximity of the United States. But the United States' invasion of Santo Domingo in 1965 revived the old pessimism, especially among the old-guard Communists. It was an illusion, they concluded, to think that the Marine mentality had been switched off in October 1962 when Kennedy promised Khrushchev not to invade Cuba if he would withdraw his missiles.

Guevara, in his contribution to the debate, grasped the importance of an American invasion. In an apathetic continent, only direct engagement on the part of the Americans would stir up the necessary nationalism that could lead to a successful revolutionary war. This, he concluded, was the lesson to be learnt from Vietnam and from Santo Domingo.

Consequently Guevara began a rural guerrilla *foco* in Bolivia that was designed eventually to bring American intervention and to spark off a continental war. The result was disaster. The *foco* theory, it can now be recognized, relied too much on the purely military aspect. Guerrilla warfare in the countryside is a desperately tough business, and all the evidence suggests that at present the counter-insurgency experts – in Latin America at least – are infinitely more adept at conducting a counter-guerrilla war than the guerrillas are at waging their own form of unorthodox warfare.

But without a proper urban organization to confuse and divert the enemy, the rural *foco* is doomed. Of course, it was never the intention of the *foco* theorists not to create such an organization. But they believed, wrongly, that it could come afterwards. Debray thought that the rural *foco* might in some way help to unite the warring factions of the Left – as to some extent happened in Cuba before 1959 – but this too seems to have been over-optimistic.

But though the details proved mistaken, the ideas of Guevara and Debray had opened up a chink in the armour of the traditional Left that left room for others to develop fresh ideas. This is the importance of Marighela. For in many ways, both Debray and Guevara were maverick figures without real roots in the orthodox Left. Neither could claim long membership of a Communist Party. But Marighela came straight out of forty years' militancy in the Brazilian Communist Party, and he ended up running the Party Committee in São Paulo, Latin America's most important industrial city – its Chicago or Manchester.

Marighela broke with the Party in 1967. He had been deeply influenced by the call to revolution that went out from Havana after the Tricontinental Conference in January 1966. And, contrary to the wishes of his Party, he attended the Havana conference of the Organization for Latin American Solidarity (OLAS), which united revolutionaries from all over the continent in July and August 1967. But this does not mean that Marighela uncritically accepted the need to set up rural *focos* throughout Brazil. It was obvious in Havana in the middle of 1967 that the Bolivian guerrilla war of Guevara was in serious trouble, and Marighela was familiar with the disastrous attempts there had already been in Brazil to start rural guerrilla movements. One of them had had to surrender after the members of the *foco* had caught bubonic plague. Though Marighela accepted the need to promote revolution, it was obvious that some different strategy was essential – certainly as far as Brazil was concerned.

In April 1964 the left-leaning government of President João Goulart had been overthrown after a military coup. This was no ordinary coup. The new military rulers had set about dismantling the old party political apparatus, imprisoned and exiled prominent political and university figures and deprived them of their political rights.

The impression given was that military rule was here to stay. This was no stop-gap military administration that would groom civilians in its image eventually to provide a respectable democratic façade. No, the military themselves were resolved to govern, irrespective of what opposition at home or abroad might say or do. Their determination became more marked as time went by and in December 1968 they went so far as to close down their own rubber-stamp Congress, thereby depriving the futuristic city of Brasília of its entire reason for existence.

The opposition to military rule, covering a wide spectrum of political belief, was at first wholly impotent to react. Virtually all the natural leaders of the Brazilian élite found themselves in prison, in exile, or forbidden to take part in politics. Students prominent in organizing demonstrations hostile to the government simply disappeared. A stringent press censorship meant that Brazilians in one city often had very little idea of what was happening in another.

Given the repression, and the massive injection of United States aid that helped to postpone any serious economic crisis, what was to be done? Some people inevitably abandoned the struggle and cultivated their garden, carving a sheltered niche for themselves and hoping that the storm would blow over. Others pinned their faith on a radicalization of the armed forces, hoping that nationalist progressive officers would arise from inside the army to lead Brazil in an anti-imperialist direction.

Carlos Marighela decided that the time had come to stand and fight, and he set about organizing that fight.

The history of the Left in Brazil has been somewhat different to that in the rest of the continent. There had been serious differences within the orthodox Communist Party in the aftermath of 1956 when several militants took exception to Khrushchev's attack on Stalin. A pro-Chinese Communist Party was set up as early as 1962, fully two years before anywhere else in the continent, and indeed before Peking itself was ready for such a move. It was founded by a group from the orthodox Brazilian Communist Party who had been expelled in 1961, and included João Amazonas, Mauricio Grabois and Pedro Pomar.

Then, in 1967, two leading members of the orthodox Party, Carlos Marighela and Mario Alves, split off on what appeared at the time to be a pro-Cuban ticket. Marighela attended the OLAS conference against the wishes of the Party, which had decided to boycott it. Early in 1968 Marighela and Alves set up the Revolutionary Communist Party of Brazil, and issued a document calling for the creation of 'a unified politico-military command' that would be designed to direct the armed struggle both in town and country.

Subsequently they launched the 'Action for National Liberation' (ALN) which was to begin the revolutionary war. At the beginning of 1969 they were joined by Captain Carlos Lamarca, who deserted from the army and founded the 'Armed Revolutionary Vanguard' (VAR). Smaller, primarily student, groups were also organized, notably the 'Revolutionary Movement October 8'. Armed revolutionary struggle began in Brazil in 1968, a struggle that was designed to start in the towns and to move inexorably to the countryside. And it possessed both a political organization and a military arm – the two indissolubly linked.

Broadly speaking Marighela's movement was pro-Cuban, but his ideological differences with the position of Guevara and Debray are well documented in this book. It is only useful to define his views in this way in order to differentiate them from other left-wing parties who were pro-Chinese or pro-Moscow. The orthodox Communist Party, for example, which held its first conference since 1960 early in December 1967 – shortly after the death of Guevara – came out in open hostility to Chinese and Cuban calls for violent revolution.

The pro-Chinese Party, on the other hand, was in favour of revolutionary war, though its position was marginally different from that of Marighela. In a document issued in December 1969 by the Central Committee of the Communist Party of Brazil (pro-Chinese), and entitled 'Intensifying the People's Struggle to fight the piratical acts of the dictatorship', the party declares clearly that liberation will involve a people's war:

It will be carried out by building a people's army and by setting up bases in the rural areas. At the same time, struggles should be carried out in various forms in the cities with the participation of the working class, the students and other sections of the people and in close combination with the armed action in the interior.

The pro-Chinese document then turns on orthodox Communists and Debrayists alike:

It is imperative to oppose the Right tendency which opposes the taking of revolutionary action on the pretext that the objective situation is not mature. At the same time, taking revolutionary action does not mean the imitation of what has been done by some petty-bourgeois groups, because their practice does not help unfold the revolutionary movement correctly. It is absolutely correct for the party to fight against the theory of guerrilla *foco* adopted under this practice. This does not mean opposition to revolutionary initiative, but to their attributing everything to the action of some small groups isolated from the people and to their denial of the necessity of a working-class party.

Finally the document called on all Party members 'to get ready to go to the interior where the people's war is to be unfolded, integrate themselves with the peasants, with the residents in the interior, raise their political consciousness, and actively unfold struggle . . .'

Although Marighela belonged to a separate organization, his position was not very far from this. He rejected the rural *foco* of Debray and Guevara, though he did not rule out guerrilla warfare in the countryside. He transferred the idea of the *foco* to the towns. Small groups of urban guerrillas, injected into the populous and potentially explosive cities of Latin America, would have a far greater impact than small bands of rural guerrillas rattling round the Brazilian jungles. But rural warfare was not excluded in Marighela's theoretical extension of the ideas of Debray. It was definitely on the agenda, and was in fact scheduled to begin late in 1969.

Revolutionary actions in the initial stages in 1968 and 1969 consisted chiefly of robbing banks in order to raise money, both for arms and for subsistence. In one year, £250,000 was stolen from fifty bank branches in São Paulo alone, and a further £150,000 in Rio. Censorship kept these figures from the Brazilians but they were reported in the foreign press.

As revolutionary activity increased, the repression became more severe. Many revolutionaries were captured, imprisoned and tortured. Consequently, when on 3 September 1969 a commando from Marighela's movement kidnapped the United States ambassador in Brazil, Mr Charles Burke Elbrick, the action was undertaken in order to secure the release of fifteen captured revolutionaries – though not all came from Marighela's group. It was an important gesture, as it focused the attention of the outside world on Brazil and for the first time brought detailed information about what was happening in Brazilian prisons. In a document left in Ambassador Elbrick's car, the kidnappers declared:

This is not an isolated act. It is another one of the innumerable revolutionary acts already carried out: bank holdups, where funds for the revolution are collected, returning what the bankers take from the people and their employees; raids on barracks and police stations, where arms and ammunitions are obtained for the struggle to topple the dictatorship; invasions of jails when revolutionaries are freed to return them to the people's struggle; the explosion of buildings that signify oppression, the execution of hangmen and torturers.

The fifteen prisoners were duly released and flown to Mexico, but the cost in terms of fresh repression was high. The death penalty, which had been abolished for seventy-five years, was reintroduced.

On 11 March 1970 the Japanese Consul-General in São Paulo, Nobuo Okuchi, was kidnapped. The liberation of five

prisoners was demanded as the price of his release. One of
them was Mother Maurina Borges da Silveira, Mother Superior
of an orphanage in Ribeirão Prêto in São Paulo state. She had
been arrested in October 1969 and kept incommunicado for a
month. After her release, she told a press conference in Mexico
City on 16 March 1970:

> I screamed when they gave me electric shocks and I prayed, but
> they laughed at me and said there would be many priests and nuns
> tortured like me and no one would help us.

In fact, not least of the remarkable aspects of the present revolutionary agitation in Brazil has been the support for the revolutionary cause of innumerable priests.

But in the wave of police activity after the kidnapping of
Ambassador Elbrick, Marighela himself was killed, on 4 November 1969. Mario Alves, his former comrade from the Communist Party, was arrested on 17 January 1970, and died some
weeks later of tortures received in the Ilha das Flôres concentration camp outside Rio de Janeiro. Marighela's second-in-
command, Joaquim Câmara Ferreira, known as 'The Old Man',
was also captured, and when Okuchi's kidnappers demanded
his release he could not be found. Jose Mariani Ferreira Alves,
Carlos Lamarca's second-in-command, was also reported captured early in 1970.

It cannot be denied that these are very serious setbacks, but
it would be wrong to conclude that armed rebellion in Brazil
has come to an end. Repression breeds discontent.

London, 1970

RICHARD GOTT

Part I

CHAPTER 1

Marighela Calls on the People to Join the Struggle

From somewhere in Brazil I am appealing to public opinion, and especially to workers, poor peasants, students, teachers, journalists, priests, bishops, youth and Brazilian women.

The military took power by violence in 1964, and they themselves prepared the way for subversion. They cannot complain or be surprised that patriots are working to dislodge them from the positions of power which they have so blatantly usurped.

What sort of order are the 'gorillas' trying to preserve? Shooting down students in the public streets? Murders by the Death Squad?* Torture and beating inside the DOPS† and military barracks?

The government has sold our country to the United States, the people's worst enemy. North Americans own the biggest estates in the country: they own a large part of Amazonia and of our mineral resources, including atomic minerals. They have missile bases at strategic points throughout our territory. North American CIA spies work here with the same facilities as in their own country, directing police searches for Brazilian patriots and supervising the government's repression of the Brazilian people.

The MEC–USAID agreement‡ has been implemented by

---

* 'Esquadrão da morte', an 'unofficial' police organization for eliminating undesirables.
† 'Department of Social and Political Order'.
‡ Agreement between the Ministry of Education and Culture and the USAID organization.

the government to establish the US education system in Brazil and turn our universities into private organizations where only the rich can study. Meanwhile there are no places in our colleges, and students must face the bullets of the military's police and fight for their education.

Workers are faced with a wage freeze and unemployment. Peasants suffer eviction, land-grabbing and rack-rents. For the North-East there is hunger, poverty and sickness.

There is no freedom in our country. Censorship is used to curtail intellectual activity.

Religious persecution grows daily; priests are arrested and exiled, bishops are threatened and attacked.

Inflation is out of control: there is too much money in the hands of wealthy capitalists while every day it is being taken out of the hands of the workers. Never have we paid so much for rents and basic necessities, and wages have never been lower.

Corruption is rife among the government. Not surprisingly the most corrupt are the ministers and military officers. Government members live like princes through contraband and theft, while civil servants are given a miserable twenty per cent pay increase.

Faced with an outrageous barrage of lies and personal insults I have no choice but to answer the government with bullets, and shall give the same answer to the police thugs who are out to take me dead or alive. This time it won't be like 64 when I was unarmed and the police fired when I couldn't hit back.*

Ultra-right-wing organizations are attacking individuals, throwing bombs, killing and kidnapping. But no one hears of the government persecuting CCC† gunmen and terrorists.

The dictatorship claims there is a subversive plot in operation, and a conspiracy among ousted politicians to overthrow the government. By mounting a witch-hunt they are out to

---

* Marighela was shot in the stomach by police while addressing a large meeting.

† 'Communist-Hunt Command': a right-wing terrorist organization.

catch the leaders of this plot. But the leader of the plot is popular discontent itself, for the people can no longer tolerate the government.

The movement which is causing so much panic in the government comes from below. It does not come from ousted politicians but from the discontented people who have opted for mass struggle.

We shall not overthrow the dictatorship with barrack-room coups, elections, re-democratization programmes or other bourgeois panaceas.

We have no faith in a parliament of yes-men set up with the dictators' blessing, and ready to yield on all demands so that the senators and deputies can keep their allowances.

We do not believe in the possibility of a peaceful solution. There is nothing artificial about the conditions of violence now existing in Brazil. They have been in existence ever since the dictatorship used force to take control.

Violence against violence. The only solution is what we are doing now: using violence against those who used it first to attack the people and nation.

The violence we are organizing and defending is that of popular armed struggle in the form of guerrilla warfare.

The 'gorillas' think the death of Che Guevara in Bolivia means the death of the guerrilla war. But inspired by the heroic example of Che Guevara we shall continue his patriotic struggle in Brazil and work with our people, confident we shall win and that history is on our side.

There is in our country a vast resistance movement against the dictatorship which has given birth to the guerrilla campaign. And in accepting the honourable title of 'public enemy number one' bestowed on me by the 'gorillas', I assume responsibility for the outbreak of guerrilla activities.

Who will launch the next attack and when, and where? These are secrets known only to the *guerrilheiros*, and the enemy will try to discover them in vain.

Revolutionary initiative is in our hands. We will act soon; we will wait no longer. The 'gorillas' will be kept in the dark until they are obliged to transform the country's present political situation into a military one.

By launching the popular revolution and using guerrilla tactics, we aim to organize a just and necessary total war against the enemies of the Brazilian people. The Brazilian revolutionary war is a long-term war, not a conspiracy. Its history has already been written with the blood of students murdered in the streets and prisons, where patriots are tortured and killed. It has been written in the activities of persecuted priests, in workers' strikes and peasant repression, and in urban and rural guerrilla warfare.

The future of the guerrilla movement depends on the revolutionary groups and the support and direct or indirect participation of the whole of the people. This is why revolutionary groups must organize from below.

Revolutionaries of all shades of political opinion and party affiliation, wherever they are, should continue the struggle and support the guerrilla movement. Since the sole duty of revolutionaries is to make the revolution, we ask no one's permission to carry out revolutionary activities and we are committed to the revolution alone.

Recent experience with popular struggle in Brazil shows that the country has entered a phase of guerrilla operations of all kinds, such as ambushes, surprise atacks, arms raids, protests and sabotage. Mass demonstrations, lightning meetings, student demonstrations, strikes, occupations, and the kidnapping of police and 'gorillas' in exchange for political prisoners are also features of our activity.

The tactical principle we must follow now is to distribute the revolutionary forces so as to intensify these methods. Later on we must concentrate the revolutionary forces for large-scale manoeuvres.

In the rural or urban area there are three types of activity for revolutionaries to choose from. They can work on the guerrilla front, the mass front or the supply front. On all these fronts work must be clandestine and secret groups must be organized with special vigilance against police infiltration, spies and double agents, who should be executed so that no information can pass to the police.

Whatever the situation, we must have arms and ammunition and increase our fire-power, and use it accurately, decisively and quickly, even in small operations like distributing leaflets and writing slogans on walls.

The popular measures we are pledged to introduce after the revolution include the following:

Abolition of privileges and censorship.

Liberty of artistic expression and religion.

Liberation of political prisoners and persons jailed by the present régime.

Liquidation of the political police, the SNI (National Information Service), CENIMAR (Marine Secret Service) and other repressive organizations.

We shall publicly try to execute CIA agents found in the country and police agents responsible for torturing, beating and shooting prisoners.

We shall expel the North Americans from the country and confiscate their property, including banks, companies and land.

We shall confiscate private Brazilian companies which collaborate with the Americans or oppose the revolution.

We shall strengthen state control of the money market, foreign trade, mineral wealth, communications and basic public services.

We shall confiscate *latifúndio** property and abolish the land monopoly; we shall guarantee property rights to the peasants who work the land, and also end such forms of exploitation as the *meia, terça parte, vale, foro, barracão*, forced evictions and *grileiros*.† We shall punish all persons responsible for crimes against the people.

We shall confiscate all fortunes illegally acquired by wealthy capitalists.

---

* *Latifúndio*: large estate which is worked by peasants and generally under-exploited.

† *Meia* and *terça*: payment of one half or one third of produce as rent; *vale, foro*: types of tenure where tenant gives owner one or two days of unpaid labour per week in lieu of money payment; *barracão*: housing and employment of labourers in squalid conditions; *grileiros*: state agents who authorize peasants to clear scrub or forest, and then take possession for themselves through forged deeds.

We shall abolish corruption.

We shall guarantee work for all men and women workers, and end unemployment and under-employment by applying the principle of 'from each according to his capacity, to each according to his work'.

We shall abolish existing legislation concerning tenancies, stop evictions, and reduce rents, as well as creating conditions where individuals can acquire their own homes.

We shall reform the education system and cancel the MEC–USAID agreement and all traces of US interference in Brazilian education, in order to orientate Brazilian education in the directions needed for the liberation of our people and the assurance of their independence.

We shall expand scientific investigation. We shall free Brazil from subservience to US foreign policy, and give firm support to the underdeveloped countries and to the anti-colonialist struggle.

These measures will be backed by the armed alliance of workers, peasants and students who will form the nucleus of the national liberation army towards which the guerrilla campaign is the first stage.

We are on the threshold of a new era in Brazil, which will be characterized by the radical transformation of Brazilian society and a realization of a new level of dignity and well-being for the men and women of Brazil.

We are struggling for power in order to substitute the bureaucratic–military state machine by the armed people. Our great objective is to form a popular revolutionary government.

Death to US imperialism.
Down with the military dictatorship.
Viva Che Guevara!

CARLOS MARIGHELA
Brazil, December 1968

CHAPTER 2

Declaration by the ALN October Revolutionary Group

To the Brazilian People:

Today revolutionary groups detained Charles Elbrick and have taken him to a place in the country where he is being held. This is not an isolated action. It is another of the innumerable revolutionary missions we have carried out, which include bank raids to finance the revolution and recover money extorted from the people by the bankers; attacks against barracks and police stations to obtain the arms and ammunition needed to overthrow the dictators; attacks on jails holding revolutionaries; sabotage of buildings connected with government repression; and execution of government executioners and torturers. In fact our kidnapping of the American ambassador is only one more operation in the revolutionary war which is progressing daily, and which this year entered its rural guerrilla stage.

By kidnapping the US ambassador we wish to demonstrate that it is possible to triumph over the dictatorship and exploitation if we are properly armed and organized. We act where the enemy expects it least and we disappear immediately, weakening the dictatorship, terrorizing exploiters and bringing the hopes of victory to the oppressed. Charles Elbrick is a representative of the imperialist interests which, allied with wealthy capitalists, landowners and bankers, are maintaining a régime based on exploitation and repression.

These groups intend to enrich themselves as much as they

can; and to do so they have introduced a wage freeze, an unjust agricultural structure and political repression. The capture of the ambassador is a clear warning to them that the Brazilian people will not let them rest, and will continue to make them feel the weight of its revolutionary action. We must all realize this is a battle without quarter which will not end merely with one general being substituted for another. The battle will end when the exploiters' régime has been replaced by a government which will rescue the working classes from their present situation.

This week is Independence Week. The people and the dictatorship are celebrating it in two different ways. The dictatorship is organizing fiestas, letting off fireworks, putting up posters. It does not really mean to celebrate anything. It wants to throw sand in the eyes of the exploited people by creating a mood of false festivity and optimism to hide the misery and oppression we are living in. But who can blot out the sun with a finger? Who can stop people seeing poverty if they are actually feeling it in their own lives?

The other Independence Week celebration is the people's, and consists of the capture of an ambassador who symbolizes repression. The life and death of the ambassador are in the dictatorship's hands. If our demands are met Elbrick will be released. If they are not we will exercise revolutionary justice.

Our two demands are:

(a) The liberation of fifteen political prisoners. They are fifteen revolutionaries among the thousands undergoing torture in prison cells throughout the country, being beaten, illtreated and humiliated by the military forces. We are not asking the impossible; we are not asking for the return to life of the countless militants who have been murdered in jail. The ones who are not freed now will one day be revenged. We are asking for the freedom of those fifteen men who directed the struggle against the dictatorship. Each of them is worth a hundred ambassadors from the people's point of view. But a US ambassador is also worth much to the dictators and exploiters.

(*b*) The publication and broadcast of this declaration, in its entirety, in the principal newspapers and on the radio and television networks of the country.

The fifteen political prisoners must be taken on a special flight to a certain country – Algeria, Chile or Mexico – where they will be given political asylum. No reprisals must be made or revenge will be taken.

The dictatorship has forty-eight hours to tell us in public whether it accepts our proposals. If the answer is positive we will deliver a list of the fifteen leaders and wait twenty-four hours for their transfer to a safe country. If the reply is negative or we receive no reply within this time-limit, we shall execute the ambassador.

The fifteen leaders must be freed, whether or not they have been formally sentenced. This is an exceptional situation, and in 'exceptional situations' the dictatorship's legal experts can usually concoct a formula to resolve problems, just as they did when the military seized power.

Negotiations can begin when the dictatorship has given public and official assurances that it will agree to our demands. Communication will always be public on the dictators' part, whereas we will choose our own time and place to make replies. We stress that the time-limit cannot be extended and we shall not hesitate to keep our promises.

Finally, here is a warning to those who torture, beat and kill our comrades. We shall not allow these atrocities to continue. This is a last warning. Anyone who persists should beware. Now it is an eye for an eye and a tooth for a tooth.

September 1969

CHAPTER 3

Greetings to the Fifteen Patriots

In the name of the ALN I send this revolutionary greeting to the fifteen patriots exchanged for the US ambassador Charles Elbrick, who was kidnapped in Rio de Janeiro in September.

We are convinced that the Brazilian people endorse this action by the ALN. This was one of the ways discovered by Brazilian revolutionaries of liberating this small group of patriots undergoing the most brutal sentences yet inflicted by the miliary fascists in Brazil. The dictatorship had no choice but to meet all the demands made by the revolutionaries. The régime published the revolutionary manifesto which denounced their crimes and their policy of national betrayal. Brazilian communications media such as radio, television and press – subject all of them to rigid censorship in Brazil – were opened to the nation and used to tell the truth to the people for the first time since 1964. Millions of Brazilians were thus able to see that the military dictatorship is torturing and murdering political prisoners.

In turn, the US government was obliged to drop appearances and give direct orders to the military junta to the effect that the dictatorship should agree to all demands in order to free their ambassador. Although the dictatorship had no alternative but to listen to the revolutionaries, it did not dare act before it had orders from the Pentagon.

There is another stronger power behind the military which takes final decisions and dictates policies to the Brazilian government. This is the power of US imperialism, whose interference in Brazil can no longer be concealed.

Thanks to intervention by the revolutionaries with an operation which has won the people's sympathy, the Brazilian dictatorship was humiliated and had to yield when confronted with our capture of the ambassador. The US government was no less humiliated because it found itself involved in events in the guise of the principal enemy of the Brazilian people.

As far as the political views of the fifteen ransomed prisoners are concerned, the revolutionaries wished to demonstrate their unanimity on two points:

(1) The dictatorship must be overthrown and the present régime transformed.

(2) The North Americans must be expelled from the country.

The road to unity is open before us. We must follow it.

What we aspire to is not simply unity among revolutionaries, but the unity of the whole Brazilian people, in order to establish a revolutionary people's government and substitute the military's bureaucratic apparatus by the armed people. We also aspire to the unity of the peoples of Latin America. Our common inspiration is the fight against US imperialism. Hence our determination to organize a just and necessary war against the military dictators and North American imperialists.

This just and necessary war has already begun in Brazil, and the kidnap of Elbrick and the freeing of the fifteen patriots are only one of its campaigns. We fully understand conditions in Brazil and in the other countries of the continent, and we declare our support for OLAS. We see our revolution as a struggle for national liberation, and as a battle to emancipate ourselves from the oligarchy and to open the way to socialism.

The Brazilian people have begun to move. They are advancing resolutely, side by side with the peoples of Latin America, with their gaze firmly fixed on the Cuban revolution, symbol of the triumph of the armed revolutionary movement.

CHAPTER 4

On the Organizational Function of Revolutionary Violence

(This work is dedicated to the New Left and to anti-fascist and revolutionary comrades in Europe.)

Our organization is the Action for National Liberation (ALN), and what it represents today was not achieved in an hour and without sacrifices, but as the result of resolute and tireless effort supported by the courage and dedication of those who died in fulfilling their revolutionary duties or were murdered by the police or taken to the reactionaries' jails and barbarously tortured.

Revolutionary action by small groups was the great enterprise which gave birth to our organization. There is no longer any doubt that it is only through revolutionary action that an organization capable of carrying the revolution through to victory can be formed.

1. EARLY REVOLUTIONARY ACTIVITY

In 1968 we were not yet a nation-wide organization, but were only a small revolutionary group in the São Paulo area and had practically nothing. We had scarcely branched out into the rest of Brazilian territory. We were starting from nothing with an initial nucleus of fighting men and women and had not yet carried out any revolutionary action capable of distinguishing us from the other numerous groups then engaged in profitless discussion. Our first step consisted in entering the struggle with an act of 'expropriation'.* Thanks to our revolutionary actions we developed our own fire-power.

Everything we achieved was the fruit of daring actions planned by small groups of revolutionaries, who began with one or two fire-arms and gradually increased their fire-power.

What made us grow was action: solely and exclusively revolutionary action. Working on the principle that action creates the vanguard, we threw ourselves into urban guerrilla warfare without yet having given it a name. The enemy, taken by surprise, supposed that our first activities were the work of bandits. As a result they lost a year following false trails. When they realized their mistake it was too late. The revolutionary war had begun.

2. REVOLUTIONARY WAR AND OUR GROWTH INTO A NATIONAL ORGANIZATION

Revolutionary warfare broke out in concrete form in the large cities of Brazil in 1968. Urban guerrilla and psychological warfare preceded rural guerrilla war.

From the start in the revolutionary war we attacked the interests of the military dictatorship, ruling classes and North American imperialism. Later we showed the ruling classes and US imperialism that we would unleash revolutionary war with all its implications on them, and take weapons and other revolutionary material from them by force. Our revolutionary strategy became clearer as our revolutionary activity grew and diversified. By expropriating from the government and powerful foreign and Brazilian capitalists, capturing arms and explosives, blocking the dictatorship's propaganda and sabotaging its activities (as in the case of the bombing of the army's anti-subversion exhibition in São Paulo), attacking the

---

* i.e. theft of arms, goods or money for revolutionary purposes. (Translators note.)

goods and property of North American imperialism and participating in joint action to punish US spies, we applied (with action, not words) a positive combat programme against the enemy. In connection with psychological warfare, we deployed the techniques of underground counter-information against the dictators, reducing them to despair. Since it has introduced censorship on all communications media, the régime has been in a constant state of tension trying to prevent the infiltration of any news which might possibly be prejudicial to the military in power. In this way we have carried out a reasonable amount of diversified action which has characterized our organization as one committed to strong action against the dictatorship and capitalism in the cause of freedom.

After this, our forces, growing continually, became much stronger. Our contacts increased in number and so did our revolutionary support. We were evolving gradually from a revolutionary group to an organization with ramifications throughout Brazil. Brazilian experience of the organizational role of action brings us to two important conclusions:

(a) A revolutionary organization establishes itself through the action it takes.

(b) What makes an organization and gives it a reputation its revolutionary action.

3. RÉSUMÉ OF OUR EARLY REVOLUTIONARY ACTIVITIES

The initiation of revolutionary action by small armed groups broke existing taboos in Brazil. Arguments rigidly defended by opportunists to the effect that conditions were not right for revolution, and that armed struggle was impossible, all fell to the ground. A year after beginning revolutionary action we can point to the following results:

(a) Our growth has been the result of revolutionary action.

(b) We have created our own fire-power.

(*c*) We have gained a year over the reactionaries, taken them by surprise with our expropriations and arms and explosive raids, and bewildered them by leaving no traces to alert them to our real intentions.

(*d*) We have diversified the activities of the war, beginning with urban guerrilla and psychological warfare – instead of with rural guerrilla warfare which would have attracted a concentration of enemy forces.

(*e*) We started at nothing, and grew into a group, then into a nation-wide organization acting in its own name and identifying its activities.

4. CLIMATE FAVOURABLE TO OUR GROWTH AND TO THE PROGRESS OF THE REVOLUTIONARY WAR

As soon as we had started urban guerrilla warfare with small armed groups, the student movement took to the streets to attack the dictators and employed street-fighting tactics which increasingly demoralized the enemy. The student movement's activities and ours converged on the same objectives and appeared united in practice. The scope of urban struggle expanded to include the whole country and the repressive forces were obliged to disperse. At that point they did not hesitate to put an end to the existing political situation and went on to establish a military dictatorship. Using the technique of the coup within the coup they made a new fascist coup on 13 December 1968 and decreed Institutional Act No. 5.

The new measures for combating revolutionary war are contained in this act, as well as in the report by Jaime Portela, government chief of military affairs, and in the new law on national security. They are fascist measures aimed against revolutionary activities, and for the first time the dictatorship has defined as revolutionary acts terrorism, bank raids, execution of foreign spies, attacks on barracks and the capture of arms and explosives. In their attempt to prevent revolutionary activity through violent laws, the enemy has become more

cruel than ever, using police terror indistinguishable from that
used by the Nazis. The cruelty of the fascists in power favoured
the climate of revolutionary warfare and created a growing
number of opponents to the Brazilian military and the present
dictatorship.

The 'gorillas' are therefore faced with a considerable increase in popular discontent and meet ever greater obstacles in
justifying policies. In such a climate our organization is gaining
ground. The December fascist coup has not checked the revolutionary war, nor have its police terror, tortures and murder
of revolutionary militants paralysed our advance.

5. THE GROWTH OF REVOLUTIONARY ORGANIZATIONS: AN ANALYSIS

There are two main ways in which revolutionary organizations
can grow. One is through propaganda and ideology – by convincing people and arguing over documents and programmes.
This method, traditional in Brazil, was typical of organizations
seeking political solutions and agreements with bourgeois personalities or groups, and its object was to confront the enemy
within the limits allowed by the régime then in power – without, in practice, any ultimate plans for its modification. In the
majority of cases militants recruited by this kind of proselytizing become disillusioned and abandon the organization
they have entered. Revolutionary organizations which devoted
themselves to proselytizing during 1966 made no advances.

The other way in which organizations grow is not through
proselytism but by unleashing revolutionary action and calling
for extreme violence and radical solutions. We prefer this way
as being more appropriate to the business of overthrowing the
dictatorship with mass strength and armed struggle than the
political juggling of personalities and bourgeois groups. When
we make use of revolutionary action, persons joining our ranks
do so because they want to fight and know they will find
nothing else but practical, genuine struggle amongst us. Since

our way is through violence, radicalism and terrorism (the only effective weapons against the dictators' violence), anyone joining our organization will not be deluded as to its real nature and will join because he has himself chosen violence.

The participation of the students in the struggle against the dictators did much to strengthen our position. During 1968 the dictatorship deployed ever-increasing fire-power against the student movement and masses and caused many casualties among street-fighters, most of whom were unarmed. Experience has shown that our tactic of using small armed groups organized for expropriations and arms capture could in fact, despite its limitations, challenge the superiority of the enemy's fire-power.

The activities of small armed groups do not rule out mass struggle and action. But they prove that without fire-power and armed men we can do nothing against the dictators.

Refusal to 'proselytize' and the concentration of our efforts on revolutionary action in order to create our own fire-power have had a decisive effect on our growth as an organization. Seeing that we were concerned with action alone, many revolutionaries who were prepared to fight to the end joined our numbers.

6. CRITICISM OF OUR ACTIVITIES IN CERTAIN REVOLUTIONARY CIRCLES

Our entrance on the Brazilian revolutionary scene with a philosophy which, since it was founded on the idea of violence and armed action against the ruling classes and North American imperialism, was openly opposed to the conventional ideas of the country's Left, and was greeted with criticisms and objections from certain revolutionary circles. They concentrated on the following points:

(*a*) We had no strategy and no idea of what to do.

(*b*) We were exclusivists and talked only of guerrilla warfare.

(*c*) We supported the idea of the *foco* and would therefore be wiped out by the reactionaries, which would damage the Brazilian revolution.

(*d*) We gave no importance to the struggle for national liberation and were thus impositive in our actions.

(*e*) We did not work amongst the masses, underestimated this sort of activity and were consequently isolated from the people.

(*f*) We were not really a revolutionary organization.

(*g*) We claimed to be fighting alone and ignored the united front.

While in 1968 the revolutionary struggle was intensifying through our practical participation, many of those who were criticizing us were falling behind because either they had no capacity for action or they made serious mistakes which brought them to the brink of disaster. What has given us the right to reject unfounded criticisms has been our revolutionary action which has been governed by a strategic plan.

7. OUR STRATEGY

We have always had a strategy, and had it been otherwise we would have never got beyond the stage of being a small group of comrades to become today a nation-wide organization. When we emerged as a group we already had a strategy and tactical programme, and our own organizational principles. All this was clearly set out in a document marking our emergence as a group and published in the first number of the *Guerrilla Fighter*, our official publication, which was launched in April 1968. The document was called 'Declaration of the Communist Group of São Paulo'. We later published a work entitled 'Some Questions on Guerrilla War in Brazil'. These contain the overall plan we have been following up to now. Readers of them will see that we have not departed from their contents. We said in them that guerrilla warfare in Brazil is the strategy for revolution and that its success depends on the rigorous execution of three phases of action: planning and preparation for guerrilla warfare, its initiation, and finally its transformation into formal war via the formation and emergence of a revolutionary army for national liberation. Working within this strategy, we have reached the current phase with urban guerrilla war under way and with preparations for rural guerrilla warfare almost complete. At the end of 1968 we surveyed our experience with revolutionary strategies and tactics in the following works: 'Operations and Tactics of Guerrilla Warfare', 'On Strategic Problems and Principles' and 'Problems of Organization'.

8. FUNDAMENTAL STRATEGIC AIMS OF OUR ORGANIZATION

From our emergence we have been careful not to conceal our revolutionary political aims. We have never failed to point out that the basic way towards conquest of power is through revolutionary war. Consequently, from our emergence as an organization and throughout its growth we have followed one line and will continue to defend the following principles:

(a) We accept the possibility of capturing power and expelling imperialism through a strategy of guerrilla warfare. In the current phase of capitalism where we are not faced with a possible world war, this is *the only valid strategy*.

(b) We accept that guerrilla warfare has definitively become a part of national life everywhere as a strategy for popular liberation. Through guerrilla warfare we shall create a revolutionary army for national liberation, the only instrument capable of annihilating the 'gorillas'' military strength. As a part of revolutionary war guerrilla warfare is the main path for armed struggle if it is to destroy the oligarchy and bring the masses to power. People who say we talk only of guerrilla warfare and are therefore exclusivists will have difficulty in concealing behind such a claim their opportunist notion of the emancipation of the Brazilian people. In fact they would accept guerrilla warfare if used merely as an instrument for achieving negotiated settlements, political agreement, elections or other conciliatory solutions of a bourgeois character. For us, on the contrary, guerrilla warfare's ultimate objective is precisely to prevent any conciliatory political negotiation with the bourgeoisie which might work against working-class and peasant interests and the Brazilian revolution, whose aim is to expel the imperialists from the country and clear the obstacles from the path to socialism.

(c) Our struggle against imperialism is being carried out with new concepts and unique techniques, and we are therefore not concerned with establishing any kind of guerrilla *foco* in Brazil. The path we are following depends on an overall strategy of developing revolutionary warfare in its three dimensions of urban guerrilla warfare, psychological war and rural guerrilla warfare. Our main effort is concentrated on rural guerrilla warfare, not through the *foco* system, but as a result of the establishment of a guerrilla infrastructure wherever our revolutionary organization appears. Given the fact that Brazil is a country of continental size, we envisage guerrilla warfare as a war of movement and not a war centred on a *foco*.

(d) The basic strategic task of Brazilian guerrilla warfare is, in our view, to liberate Brazil and expel North American imperialism. Our struggle is a struggle for national liberation and is simultaneously against the oligarchy and against the capitalists.

The principal enemy of our people is North American capitalism. But bearing in mind the close ties between North American imperialism and the big capitalists and *latifundiários* of Brazil, the country cannot be liberated without these capitalists and *latifundiários* being, at the same time, driven out of power, and replaced by the armed people and a popular revolutionary government.

9. WORK AMONG THE MASSES AND RELATIONS WITH THE PEOPLE

In the current situation in Brazil, revolutionaries are divided between two distinct concepts of political work among the masses and of relations with the people.

The first is the one held by organizations who concentrate on short-term demands and thereby try to win the masses for the revolution. But the military dictatorship will not listen to demands and uses against them laws and emergency decrees and, above all, an increasing fire-power which it will not hesitate to use to shoot down street demonstrators. Organizations which limit their activities simply to working with the masses, formulating demands in the hope of transforming this into a political struggle, are finally rendered helpless by the armed superiority of the enemy.

The other concept of mass political work is held by organizations whose basic concern is armed struggle aimed at returning the dictatorship's fire with arms which, although small in quantity, are handled by revolutionaries and mass movements. The masses coalesce round this fire-power as it emerges and expands, build their unity around it and march on to power. The essence of this concept consists in maintaining the importance of mass movements as a function of armed struggle. According to this point of view, the mass movement cannot survive unless it is supported by fire-power coming from the revolutionaries. Consequently we cannot be accused of underestimating mass movements on the grounds that we hold such views as these.

In politics one must evaluate the correctness of a position by its results among the people. Organizations doing nothing due to the impossibility of a struggle based on mass demands are falling behind and being forgotten. Organizations – like ours – which use violence and armed struggle are the ones which achieve results and win the sympathy and confidence of the masses and link themselves to the people.

10. REVOLUTIONARY CHARACTER OF OUR ORGANIZATION

The fact that our organization is revolutionary in character is due above all to the fact that all our activity is revolutionary. Our methods and organizational forms are governed by our revolutionary activity and we accept nothing that could hinder or limit this activity.

We have kept our organization free from complex command systems depending on internal hierarchies and a numerous and immobile bureaucracy at the top. Our basic function is not to hold meetings but to act – for which rigorous planning is always required.

In our organization it is necessary to plan all operations well beforehand in order not to hesitate once we are under way and to complete the operation successfully. We never undertake operations unless we have determination to succeed and certainty that success is possible, nor do we undertake any operation light-heartedly or out of exhibitionism. Our organization relies heavily on its revolutionary groups and its fire-power, on men equipped to handle that fire-power and to carry out the operations and tactics required by popular armed struggle.

There is no distinction within our ranks between politicians and military. In the Brazilian revolutionary war we do not have political commissars watching over military cadres. All members of the organization necessarily fulfil both functions and are prepared for this from the start. Those who cannot cope with the dual role of combatant and politician are ill equipped to survive in our organization, for this is our way of acting. The problem is the same for those working on our mass front and logistics front. These two have considerable importance in revolutionary warfare, and militants in them must strive to acquire political and military knowledge, however elementary, to keep up with the movement's development and apply its line.

These organizational principles and techniques which we apply in practice leave no doubt as to the revolutionary character of our organization.

11. REVOLUTIONARY ACTION AND UNITED FRONT

We are not the only organization now fighting in Brazil. Other organizations include armed struggle in their programmes. Although there are in our country so many organizations preaching armed struggle, guerrilla warfare only emerged as something tangible when we decided to use the tactic of small armed groups as initiators of revolutionary action.

Unlike other countries where armed struggle is or has been in progress, revolutionary armed struggle did not, in Brazil, issue from the united front. For Brazilian revolutionaries the united front is a necessity. But in our case, thanks to the diversity of circumstances and policies among revolutionary organizations, the united front was an impossibility until the first armed revolutionary action had been taken.

For our part we have fulfilled our revolutionary duty and have gone into battle in the urban areas with our weapons even though people had accused us of rashness and hastiness. Once the struggle is under way the road to revolution is open. With the fire-power the Brazilian revolutionaries now dispose of, it is possible to achieve a united front. The creation and strengthening of revolutionary fire-power, together with its continued activity, is what will cause the revolutionaries' armed forces to coalesce and unite. United front is fire-power; it is revolutionary action – and nothing else.

On the other hand, our organization is not in itself a united front. Its structures, discipline, techniques and principles are distinct from the united front's. To create that united front we are ready to make every effort, and this is why we are striving to increase our fire-power and the amount of revolutionary activity we have carried out. We have also systematically worked to spread our point of view in order to consolidate a

united front, and it is with this intention that we are pursuing
armed struggle in our country.

12. SHORTCOMINGS OF THE BRAZILIAN REVOLUTIONARY MOVEMENT AND PROSPECT FOR THE STRUGGLE IN OUR COUNTRY

The overwhelming defect of the Brazilian revolutionary movement is the disunited state of the revolutionary organizations
and their disagreement over attitudes and objectives. Within
this disagreement there is an intense struggle for leadership
going on. Each organization is tacitly claiming the leadership of
the revolution for itself, and this makes it difficult to discover a
common denominator among those who are prepared to fight
against our common enemy. This is an objective feature of the
Brazilian revolution and of the special conditions in which it is
evolving.

It is hard to discover truth except in practice. We had to
resort to action in order to achieve some results. Once the
armed struggle was initiated with small groups of revolutionaries in the urban area, the business of selecting organizations
capable of concrete action began. There are still some people
arguing over the leadership question, but now, when we have
already taken up our weapons for the fight, it is impossible to
hope to play any leading role with the sort of argument usually
conducted about subjective programmes, and with doctrinaire
positions divorced from Brazilian social reality.

In the continuing dispute for the leadership, there is now
circulating in Brazil a thesis which says that he who fires the
first shot takes the others with him. This mistaken idea has
frequently caused some organizations at this stage of the
struggle to commit hasty actions for which they were unprepared or unsuited at the time. This kind of mistake is usually
fatal and invariably leads to imprisonment, loss of men and
arms and even annihilation of groups and organizations. The
question in Brazil does not revolve around the first-shot myth.

We must realize that the first shot has already been fired, since we are already in the middle of a developing revolutionary war. The crucial problem for us is to ensure that everyone does his duty, and every revolutionary's duty is to make the revolution.

No revolutionary organization wins the leadership simply by calling itself leader or assuming the functions of leadership. Before we can decide the indispensable leadership of the Brazilian revolution, we must increase the amount of revolutionary activity until we reach a point where we strike a hard blow at the bureaucratic–military machine of the Brazilian state. This objective cannot be attained through the activities of a single organization.

Another shortcoming of the Brazilian revolution is its inexperience. The revolutionary movement in our country is young. Its recent past dates from 1968 when urban guerrilla warfare was begun. It is also a movement in which the overwhelming majority of supporters are young people of both sexes. Besides Brazilian women, who up to then played no part in revolutionary activities but have joined in, its members include students, workers, peasants, intellectuals, artists, and men of the liberal professions. All of these have been confronted only with the complex and serious problems raised by revolution since 1968. They are problems arising from a kind of struggle with which we are unfamiliar, i.e. the problem of facing the enemy with our weapons in our hands, starting from a situation in which we have nothing, neither arms nor means. Inexperience has led to some errors and failures, our organization not excepted. Both error and failure are sources of experience, and although mistakes should be avoided, when they happen we should know how to draw the right conclusions from them.

The revolutionary movement in our country is also suffering from shortages on the technical front, and lacks men with trained knowledge of modern weapons and their use. The technical training of combatants is not achieved in a moment; it requires time and it is this factor which prevents us from making faster headway and transforming our struggle against dictatorship and US imperialism as urgently as we need to.

The outlook in Brazil is one of prolonged struggle in which there can be no short cuts or time-limits. We are beginning the revolutionary struggle with a slow but methodical urban guerrilla war directed against the interests of big foreign and Brazilian capitalists, causing uncertainty and insecurity among the ruling classes and wearing down and demoralizing the 'gorillas'' military forces.

From the urban front we shall go on to direct armed struggle against the *latifúndio* through rural guerrilla warfare. With the armed alliance of proletariat, peasantry and students in a decentralized and mobile guerrilla war, we shall extend our activities in all directions through the interior of Brazil and finally create a revolutionary army of national liberation to match the conventional army of the military dictatorship.

The conquest of power and the establishment of the popular revolutionary government are our two great objectives. After this we shall throw the North Americans out of the country. We shall confiscate Brazilian companies or concerns which collaborate with the North Americans. We shall confiscate *latifúndio* property and push the agrarian revolution through to its conclusion, thus liberating the peasantry. We shall free Brazil from its condition as a satellite of the military blocs, and follow a policy of total support for the underdeveloped peoples and struggle against colonialism.

May 1969

CHAPTER 5

Problems and Principles of Strategy

The Brazilian revolution's most important problem is its strategy, and on this point – i.e. on the question of its ultimate direction – there is no complete agreement among revolutionaries. Our organization adopted a certain strategy and has been guided by it; but it is obvious that other organizations hold different points of view.

The principles expounded here therefore concern questions on which our organization can give opinions based on its own experience. For us the strategy of the Brazilian revolution lies in guerrilla warfare. Guerrilla war is a part of the people's revolutionary war. In 'Some Questions on Guerrillas in Brazil' we set down the principles underlying our strategy, and those interested need only to refer to this work. To the principles listed there we would like to add others which will help to give an idea of our strategic thinking about the Brazilian revolution.

Study and practical application of these principles by revolutionary groups and the personal experience of militant revolutionaries may contribute to a better understanding not only of the objectives of our struggle but of the basic means we use to achieve them. The following are the strategic principles in question:

1. STRATEGY OF THE ALN

(*a*) In a country like Brazil, suffering from a permanent political crisis resulting from the worsening of the chronic structural crisis in the country and the general crisis of capitalism, and where military rule has been established as a consequence, our strategic aim is to *convert the political crisis into armed struggle by the people against the military powers*.

(*b*) The basic principle of revolutionary strategy in a context of permanent political crisis is to unleash, in urban and rural areas, a volume of revolutionary activity which will oblige the enemy to transform the country's political situation into a military one. Then discontent will spread to all social groups and the military will be held exclusively responsible for failures.

(*c*) The main aim of the revolutionary strategy, when the permanent political crisis has been transformed into armed struggle and the political situation into a military one, is to annihilate the bureaucratic–military machine of the state and replace it by the armed people.

(*d*) In pursuing this objective, the revolutionary strategy's basic premise is that, in the present conditions of political crisis, the bureaucratic–military machine of the Brazilian state is maintaining ever closer relations with North American imperialist interests. This state machine cannot be destroyed unless the main blow is directed against North American imperialism, which is the common enemy of humanity, and primarily of the peoples of Latin America, Asia and Africa.

(*e*) In our view revolutionary strategy is a total strategy, both in the sense that it opposes the global strategies of US imperialism, and in the sense that it includes both political and military strategy as an indivisible unity and not as two separate activities. Moreover, tactics must be a function of strategy and there is no possibility of deploying tactics which do not serve a strategy.

(*f*) Given the total nature of our strategy we must, in initiating the struggle against the military dictatorship, realize that a radical change of Brazilian class structures in a socialist direction is a principle of strategy. Simultaneously, our principle enemy is North American imperialism and we must transform the struggle against imperialism into a national anti-oligarchy liberation struggle.

Faced with revolutionary attacks, the military powers will be obliged to come to the defence of North American imperialism and the Brazilian oligarchy, and thus lose prestige with the people. On the other hand, by destroying the military's political power and armed forces, we shall expel the North Americans from the country and eradicate the Brazilian oligarchy, thus clearing away the obstacles lying in the path towards socialism.

2. STRATEGIES OF URBAN AND RURAL STRUGGLE

(a) The city is the area of complementary struggle, and the whole urban struggle whether on the guerrilla or mass-movement front, must always be seen as tactical struggle.

(b) The decisive struggle will be in the rural area – the strategic area – and not in the tactical area (i.e. the city).

(c) If, by some error, urban struggle were conducted as if it were decisive in strategic terms, the strategic struggle in the rural area would be relegated to a secondary place. Once the bourgeoisie notices the weakness or absence of peasant participation in the struggle, it will take advantage of this to sabotage the revolution. In other words it will try to side-track the proletariat if the latter is not supported by the peasantry – its fundamental ally – and will try to preserve the state's bureaucratic and military apparatus.

(d) Only when the reactionaries' armed forces have been liquidated, and the bourgeoisie's military apparatus is no longer capable of acting against the masses, should a general strike be used in the cities to support the guerrilla war in its last stages before final victory. This principle must be applied in order to prevent the bourgeoisie subverting the general strike and launching a coup to block the revolution and prevent its taking power.

3. URBAN GUERRILLA STRATEGY

(a) Since the city is the area of tactical support struggle, urban guerrilla forces play a tactical role in support of the rural guerrilla movement. Consequently we must use urban activity as a diversionary technique to create tension and side-track the armed forces to stop them concentrating their repressive operations on the rural guerrilla.

(b) In urban guerrilla warfare our techniques are not those of mass struggle, but of small armed groups with their own fire-power acting against the dictatorship. When they realize that the revolutionaries' fire-power is being directed against their enemies, the masses – hitherto helpless against the dictatorship – will recognize the *guerrilheiros* as their ally and come to their support.

(c) Urban guerrilla techniques are composed of guerrilla tactics and armed activities of all kinds such as ambushes and surprise attacks, expropriations, arms and explosives raids, revolutionary terrorism, sabotage, occupation of or attacks on property, punishment of North American spies or police torturers, lightning meetings, pamphlet distribution and slogan-writing by armed groups or others.

(d) Both urban and rural guerrilla warfare need to be backed by a campaign for training guerrilla fighters, increasing their physical strength and self-defence skills, and teaching them to use their professional skills to manufacture home-made arms etc. Guerrilla forces must also create and strengthen their own fire-power and ability to use it, and set up information networks, communications and transport services and medical and first-aid facilities. Our technique is to count on the support and supply system of both urban and rural sections of the guerrilla movement in order not to be reduced to rural or urban guerrilla activity alone, and to maintain a correct combination of both.

(e) Revolutionaries involved in guerrilla war give enormous importance to the urban mass movement and its activities such as strikes, marches, protests, boycotts etc. Our strategic approach to the urban mass movement is to participate in it with the intention of creating a support system for working-class armed struggle, in order to be able to deploy urban and other guerrilla forces with larger armed groups.

4. RURAL GUERRILLA STRATEGY

(*a*) Conflicts in peasant areas arising from demands against *latifundiários*, or from rural syndicates or unions, can develop into armed conflicts and thus have positive value. It is unlikely, however, that rural guerrilla warfare of a strategic nature will arise out of conflicts originating in peasant demands alone. The Brazilian peasantry has limited political awareness, and traditionally its struggle has taken the form of banditry and mysticism; its experience of class struggle under proletarian direction is both new and limited.

Given current Brazilian post-dictatorship conditions, a strategic struggle in the rural area will evolve out of a guerrilla infrastructure created among the peasantry. Once they see the creation in their midst of armed groups working against *latifundiários* and favourable to peasant interests, they will support the guerrilla movement and join it.

(*b*) The point to stress about guerrilla struggle is that it can have no decisive importance in the revolutionary war unless the armed alliance of workers and peasants is consolidated and supported by the students. This alliance, equipped with growing fire-power, will give the guerrilla war firm foundations and assure its eventual success. Armed alliance between proletariat, peasantry and middle-class groups is the key to victory.

(*c*) Rural guerrillas are crucial because, besides being extremely mobile throughout the whole continental area of Brazil and leading ultimately to the formation of a revolutionary national liberation army, they conduct a type of warfare which can be organized round an embryo of armed peasants, proletariat and students. The peasantry – without which the revolution cannot be successfully completed – cannot be incorporated into the urban guerrilla struggle.

(d) At no point should the Brazilian guerrilla movement defend any territory or region or any fixed base. If we do this we allow the enemy to concentrate his forces, surround and annihilate known and vulnerable targets.

(e) Brazilian rural guerrillas must always be mobile. Similarly, urban guerrillas must always be extremely mobile and we must never occupy any point without having meticulously prepared our retreat in advance. Revolutionary war is a war of movement, whatever the situation in Brazil.

(f) Guerrilla war is a part of revolutionary war and plays the main strategic role within it; its ultimate political aim is to create a national liberation army and to take power. We must avoid any distortion of this objective in the course of the revolutionary struggle, prevent urban or rural guerrilla groups degenerating into banditry, and beware of joining with bandits or using their methods.

5. ORGANIZATIONAL STRATEGY

(a) The continental size of Brazil and the widely varying strategic importance of its regions, together with the principle of diversity of revolutionary activity, will determine, on a regional basis, where revolutionary centres will form and how they should be coordinated. Such revolutionary centres will devote themselves to creating a guerrilla organization and to launching revolutionary struggle, and will have freedom of tactical and political action on a regional basis.

(b) The strategic and tactical leadership of our organization – i.e. the overall military leadership – will not emerge immediately, nor will it be fixed once and for all. It will shape itself through a continuous process in which armed struggle and guerrilla warfare will be primary and will continue until a group of men and women totally identified with the revolutionary struggle emerges capable of carrying it to its conclusion.

(c) The revolutionary unity of our organization exists in terms of the strategic and tactical principles we apply and not in terms of names or personalities. It is this identity of ideology, both theoretical and practical, which will ensure that revolutionaries scattered throughout the country will carry out activities which will identify them as belonging to the same organization.

January 1969

CHAPTER 6

Questions of Organization

Our organization was created to apply a practical revolutionary policy with guerrilla war as its strategy. The principles of the organization are quite distinct from those of traditional left-wing organizations in Brazil, whose functions revolved round meetings to discuss documents and conduct other more or less bureaucratic business dictated to them by the leaders and never put into practice.

On the contrary, our organization is run from below and is based on revolutionary action carried out primarily by the revolutionary groups on which our organization is based. The small initial group of combatants worked to construct an infrastructure which would enable them to act, instead of worrying about building a hierarchical organization through meetings of delegates or by calling together leaders from the old conventional political groups.

1. INITIAL STRUCTURE OF OUR ORGANIZATION

In view of this, our organization relied at the outset on a small group devoted to secret guerrilla activities and to constructing a guerrilla training centre. This latter branch of our organization is mobile in character, since its function in the organization responds to the immediate interests and demands of guerrilla strategy, and it must undergo complex dismantling and relocation operations.

Our group consisted primarily of this group and local revolutionary groups of two kinds:

(*a*) Groups derived from the transformation of older, conventional organizations into revolutionary groups.

(*b*) Non-conventional groups of a non-party nature who opted for our methods and joined our ranks.

On the basis of groups already in existence we built our urban organization, which later grew with the creation of other kinds of groups as the movement evolved. At the same time other small, autonomous revolutionary groups engaged in revolutionary activities, for example ecclesiastics and individual revolutionaries, decided to join our organization.

2. CHANGES ARISING FROM THE FORMATION OF SPECIALIZED GROUPS, AND THEIR IMPORTANCE

Our organizational principles are not static or dogmatic, since Marxism–Leninism teaches that no organization is abstract. In our view organizations always serve a political purpose, and changes in the nature of the revolutionary movement cause changes in the revolutionary organization. As the revolutionary movement progressed changes were introduced in the organization. In turn, certain changes of an organizational nature influenced the movement's development. In our organization a change occurred when the guerrilla training centre started to produce results and provide groups for strategic and tactical tasks and to reinforce local activity. In future our concern that the training centre should take priority will improve the quality of personnel available and this should produce rewarding results. This may bring a new change in our revolutionary organization and in the form and content of our guerrilla activities, as well as in our local activities.

3. MOBILE UNITS

Another change in our organization resulted from the formation of two mobile units: the strategic task force and the armed tactical group. The task force and tactical group carried out essential activities, working independently from each other with scarcely a link between them. The tactical group was a great support for the strategic group. It increased its fire-power considerably and carried out important attacks on enemy positions, and with its special experience and aptitude for active combat it will very soon enable us to launch an open struggle against the dictatorship in the strategic area – i.e. in the countryside.

The armed tactical group represents a crucial stage in our organization: we have moved from a situation where we had nothing and no fire-power to a situation where we dispose of reasonable fire-power. This fact alone shows we have made a leap forward in revolutionary terms. The group is a special instrument for the most complex operations which need the heaviest concentration of fire-power. The management of this fire-power needs more specialized technical knowledge, which makes the tactical group into a specialized section. For this reason the tactical group cannot be identified with technically less prepared revolutionary groups not possessing great fire-power or the means to carry out subversive activity. The recruitment area for the armed tactical group is among the most militant and determined revolutionaries and revolutionaries who have already seen action and are ready to be transferred to the tactical group and accept the consequences arising from their changed situation.

4. CREATION OF THE THREE FRONTS

As far as the activity of the local groups was concerned, the new factor which emerged and caused a change in our organization was the division of our activity in 1968 into three fronts: the guerrilla front, the mass front and the support network.

This three-front division was typical of our local activity throughout the country. Since, however, the revolutionary movement is characteristic in that it develops unevenly in different parts of the country, it happened that in some areas one or other of these fronts disappeared or developed much more strongly than the other two. Our next objective in connection with local activity is to ensure that the three fronts develop evenly throughout the country and that they should all be equally effective. The combination of the three fronts should result in the intensification of the guerrilla war.

5. THE GUERRILLA FRONT

The guerrilla front normally undertakes arms and explosives raids, revolutionary terrorism, sabotage, armed missions and other anti-imperialist activities. It also performs operations like wall-painting and leaflet distribution, organizes lightning meetings and also operates the clandestine anti-dictatorship press.

The guerrilla front is built on an infrastructure or underground system based on the manufacture and production of arms and home-made sabotage devices. With supplies of captured arms, this infrastructure is one of the decisive factors in changing the nature of the revolutionary movement and its organization. A guerrilla front which is constantly expanding must even go as far as a burnt-earth policy to create alarm among the dictators, and divert a large part of their forces to prevent them from pursuing their anti-guerrilla campaign.

At every point in the country local activity must count on the existence of a guerrilla front and the efforts of local revolutionary organizations should be channelled towards its formation.

6. THE MASS FRONT

The mass front, led by the student movement, played an unprecedented part in the struggle against the dictatorship. Occupations, demonstrations, protests, strikes, anti-censorship activities, capture of policemen and exchange of prisoners; all these represented mass-struggle techniques of a very high order. Continued activity by local revolutionary groups among workers, peasants and other exploited groups will mean a great step forward in the anti-dictatorship struggle. Here the part played by students and ecclesiastics is especially significant; it demonstrates that the Brazilian middle classes repudiate the dictatorship and have become one of the most militant forces in the current revolutionary process.

The mass front requires the organization of revolutionary groups in places of work and study both in city and rural areas. On top of this we must equip the mass front with adequate fire-power. Mass-movement activities should be armed activities, and an infrastructure similar to the guerrilla movement's should be set up on the mass front. Above all we should concentrate on establishing this infrastructure among the rural masses, in view of the need for a radicalization of the struggle in this area.

We should not confuse 'mass front' with work among the masses. The mass front is a combat front, an action front going as far as armed action. Work among the masses is the business of creating political consciousness and infiltrating the masses via cultural media, and generating demands among the people. Revolutionaries do not despise these means, but they do not confuse them with the mass front.

7. SUPPORT NETWORK

This is the great logistics front behind the Brazilian revolution and guerrilla war. Here too revolutionary infrastructures are necessary, as well as individual and collective support in the cities and – above all – in the countryside. Houses, addresses, hiding-places, financial resources, supplies, information – these are the things the support front needs, and the formation of this network deserves special attention from the revolutionaries.

8. CHARACTERISTICS OF OUR PRESENT ORGANIZATION

Due to changes in the organization, its structure has evolved from its previous form and is now characterized by the following main features:

(*a*) We have a strategic command concerned with the problems of rural guerrilla warfare, with secret strategic affairs and also with managing the combat training centre.

(*b*) We have mobile units such as the strategic task-force and tactical armed group. These units are under the direction of the strategic command of rural guerrilla activities, and they have no fixed radius of action, working wherever the strategic command decides.

(*c*) In each important urban area we have a regional coordination group. The regional group maintains a support system for the armed struggle and is responsible for urban guerrilla activities. It creates the fire-power required for urban guerrilla warfare and manages the three revolutionary fronts for the urban area under its control. If necessary the regional command can establish smaller groups to complement the armed organization and intensify urban guerrilla warfare.

The regional command does not maintain any permanent contact with mobile units under the direction of the strategic command, thus avoiding a situation where everyone knows about everything and everybody. Direct contact with the regional command is maintained with the strategic command via the communications network.

(*d*) Small autonomous organizations and individual revolutionary militants and free-shooters join our organization with absolute freedom of action providing they accept, defend and fulfil without reservation all our strategic and tactical principles.

(*e*) The backbone of our organization are the revolutionary groups which possess qualities of combativeness and initiative. The revolutionary groups have the right to reject anyone who, in the name of the strategic command, attempts to check any revolutionary initiative which is in line with the strategic and tactical principles of the organization.

(*f*) In our organization there is no complex chain of command, and this is intended to guarantee organizational simplicity and ensure rapidity of action, mobility and local initiative. Neither do we have political commissars or supervisors such as exist in other organizations; everything is based on the correct application of our guiding principles and the combative initiative of the revolutionaries.

(*g*) Leadership in our organization and in the regional groups is very simple in structure and consists of a small number of comrades who must win confidence by outstanding participation in the most dangerous and responsible activities, and by their intransigence in the defence and application of our principles.

9. A NEW EXPERIMENT IN REVOLUTIONARY ORGANIZATION AND LEADERSHIP

With this type of revolutionary organization we are in fact confronting a unique experiment in the Brazilian revolutionary movement. Consequently there are still problems regarding our national activities which can only be resolved when we have advanced still further with guerrilla tactics and operations. In no circumstances, although liberty of political and revolutionary action are indispensable for the functioning of the local organizations, is revolutionary leadership spontaneous. Leadership is the direct result of mobile strategic and tactical action of a comprehensive kind plus the greatest possible volume of efficient and technically well-organized firepower.

10. OUR PRINCIPLES

(a) The basic aim of our organization is a launch guerrilla warfare; and once it is under way to make the organization the instrument of a political line depending on this strategy.

(b) For an organization to be revolutionary it must practise revolution on a permanent basis, but it can never abandon its strategic concepts, ideological principles and internal discipline.

(c) A revolutionary organization does not become the vanguard simply by giving itself the name. To be the vanguard it must act and accumulate a fund of convincing revolutionary activity, since action alone makes the vanguard.

(d) Our principal activity is not the construction of a party but to launch revolutionary action.

(e) The basic thing in a revolutionary organization is not to call futile meetings on generalized bureaucratic topics but to dedicate oneself systematically to planning and executing every possible kind of revolutionary activity.

(f) The decisive moving force in the movement is the initiative of its revolutionary groups.

(g) We do not have a separate military policy subordinated to the political. Our policy is a total revolutionary policy combining military and political policy as a single entity.

(h) The guerrilla movement is not the armed section of any political movement. The guerrilla movement itself leads the revolution.

(i) What determines the creation and growth of the political leadership is revolutionary action and its success, and the decisive, constant, personal participation of the leadership in this action.

(j) There is no leadership without sacrifice and direct participation in revolutionary activity. Political leadership has no status, nor does it signify any recognition of hierarchy or grades of importance in the various functions occupied by revolutionaries. The various posts and positions have no value in themselves. In the revolutionary organization only missions and operations have value.

(*k*) The duty of all revolutionaries is to make the revolution.

(*l*) We ask no one's permission or authorization to make the revolution.

(*m*) We are committed only to the revolution.

(*n*) The limits of our organization are the limits of its influence and revolutionary capacities.

(*o*) The foremost task of the revolutionary organization is to guard against the class enemy and the police as closely as possible. Informers, spies, stooges and traitors of all kinds must suffer exemplary punishment.

(*p*) Our basic security rule is that each one should know only as much as concerns his work. Otherwise it is impossible to guarantee the clandestine nature of the organization.

Brazil, December 1968

CHAPTER 7

Handbook of Urban Guerrilla Warfare

In presenting this book, I should like to pay a twofold homage: first, to the memory of Edson Luis Souto, Marco Antonio Brás de Carvalho, Nelson José de Almeida, 'Escoteiro',* and so many other urban guerrillas and fighters murdered by the political police (DOPS) and army of the military dictatorship now controlling Brazil; secondly, to our brave comrades, men and women, rotting their lives away in government gaols, and subjected to tortures which the Nazis themselves might envy. Like theirs, our one and only duty is to fight.

INTRODUCTION

Anyone who opposes the military dictatorship and wants to fight against it can do something, however little. To anyone who reads this handbook, and then decides he can no longer remain inactive, I can only urge that he follow the instructions I suggest, and join the struggle at once. For by any hypothesis, and under whatever circumstances he may find himself, the duty of a revolutionary is to make the revolution.

While it is important to read this pamphlet, it is equally desirable to pass it on. I hope that everyone who accepts the ideas he finds in it will get more copies duplicated or printed, even if he needs the protection of an armed group to do it.

The reason I have signed it is that it contains the sys-

* 'Boy Scout'.

tematized results of the experiences of a group of men who have fought under arms in Brazil, of which I had the privilege to be one. To those who cast doubt on my recommendations, and still affirm that the right conditions do not yet exist for fighting – or who simply deny the facts described here – I can only say that it is best for me openly to admit responsibility for what I have said and done. I therefore reject the doubtful convenience of anonymity.

My object is to recruit as many supporters as possible. The words 'aggressor' and 'terrorist' no longer mean what they did. Instead of arousing fear or censure, they are a call to action. To be called an aggressor or a terrorist in Brazil is now an honour to any citizen, for it means that he is fighting, with a gun in his hand, against the monstrosity of the present dictatorship and the suffering it causes.

What is an urban guerrilla?

The chronic crisis in all our structures which characterizes the situation of Brazil, together with the resulting political instability, have helped in launching the revolutionary war, a war which may take the form of urban guerrilla activity, rural guerrilla activity, or psychological warfare. The task of the urban guerrilla in the cities is to fight both the guerrilla and the psychological battles, and it is with him that I am concerned here.

The urban guerrilla is an armed man who uses other than conventional means for fighting against the military dictatorship. As a political revolutionary and also a convinced patriot, he is struggling to set his country free, and is thus a friend of its people and their liberty. His battlefield consists of the major cities of our country.

There are also bandits in the cities, normally considered in Brazil as outlaws; and it can happen that attacks made by them are thought to be the work of guerrillas. The two are, however, totally different. The outlaw is concerned only with his personal advantage, and will quite indiscriminately attack exploiters and exploited – thus claiming many of the poorest as his victims. The urban guerrilla, on the other hand, is struggling for a political purpose, and attacks only the government, the large capitalists, and imperialist agents, especially North Americans.

As well as such outlaws, there are other equally harmful elements at work in our cities: the right-wing counter-revolutionaries, who create confusion, rob banks, kidnap or murder guerrillas, revolutionary priests, students, and other citizens who hate fascism and love freedom. The urban guerrilla is an implacable enemy of the government, and systematically works against the authorities, and those who rule the country and wield power. His major job is to baffle, discredit and harass the military and other forces of repression, and to destroy or loot goods belonging to North Americans, the heads of foreign firms, or the Brazilian upper classes.

The urban guerrilla is not afraid of dismantling and destroying the present economic, political and social system, for his objective is to further the rural guerrilla war, and so contribute to the establishment of completely new and revolutionary social and political structures, in which the people will be armed and in power.

The urban guerrilla must have a certain minimum political understanding. It would be helpful for him to try to read the following:

> *Guerrilla War*, by Che Guevara*
> *Some Questions about the Brazilian Guerrillas*
> *Guerrilla Operations and Tactics*†
> *Problems and Principles of Stragegy*†
> *Some Tactical Principles for Comrades Carrying Out Guerrilla Operations*
> *Matters of Organization*†
> *The Role of Revolutionary Action in Organization*†
> *O Guerrilheiro*, the newssheet of the Brazilian revolutionary groups.

* Penguin Books, 1969.
† Published in the Nov. 1969 number of *Temps modernes*.

THE PERSONAL QUALITIES AN URBAN GUERRILLA MUST HAVE

The urban guerrilla is characterized by courage and a spirit of initiative. He must be a good tactician and a good shot, and make up for his inferiority in weapons, ammunition and equipment by his skill and cunning.

The career soldier or the policeman has modern arms and good vehicles at his disposal, and can travel freely wherever he wishes, since the whole power structure supports him. The urban guerrilla, lacking such resources, has to act secretly. He may even be under condemnation of death, or a prison sentence, in which case he will have to have false identity papers.

The urban guerrilla does, however, have one enormous advantage over both the conventional soldier and the policeman: he is defending a just cause, the cause of the people – whereas they are on the side of an enemy the people hate.

Though his arms are inferior to those of his enemy, his moral superiority is incontestable, and it is this which enables him to carry out his major tasks: to attack and to survive.

In order to be able to fight at all, the urban guerrilla must be able to capture arms from the enemy. Since he may do this under widely differing circumstances, he will find himself with a somewhat varied collection of weapons for which he lacks the appropriate ammunition. The urban guerrilla has nowhere to practise marksmanship either; but these are all problems he will conquer by using his imagination and creativity – two indispensable qualities for a successful revolutionary.

The urban guerrilla must have a spirit of initiative; he must be mobile, flexible, able to adapt to circumstances, and able to keep a cool head; the most important of these qualities is the spirit of initiative, for one cannot always foresee exactly what will happen, and the guerrilla has no time to waste wondering what to do, or expecting someone else to tell him. He must act, working out a suitable solution for each problem as it presents itself, without hesitation. It is better to act mistakenly than do nothing for fear of doing wrong; you cannot be an urban guerrilla without a spirit of initiative. Other qualities are also desirable: you must be a good walker, resistant to fatigue, hunger, rain and heat; you must be able to hide and keep watch, know the arts of disguise, never be intimidated by danger, act as easily by night as by day – but never precipitately – possess unlimited patience, keep calm and clearheaded in even the worst predicaments, never leave a trace behind you, and never be discouraged.

Some guerrillas, faced with difficulties which seemed to them almost insurmountable, have weakened, and disappeared or resigned.

Urban guerrilla activity is not like a business deal, or working on the shop floor, or staging a play. It demands the same kind of commitment as rural guerrilla activity, and anyone lacking in the necessary qualities would do better not to attempt it.

HOW THE URBAN GUERRILLA LIVES

The urban guerrilla must be able to live among other people without appearing in any way different from anyone else. He must not dress flamboyantly – eccentric or extremely fashionable clothes in a working-class district would be too noticeable. Similarly, costume varies between north and south, and care must be taken over that too. He must earn his living, doing an ordinary job.

If he is wanted by the police, or known to them, if he is under sentence of death or imprisonment, then he may have to go into hiding and live in secrecy.

Whatever the circumstances, the urban guerrilla must never speak of his activities to anyone; they concern only the revolutionary organization he belongs to. He must have a great capacity for observation, and be very well informed, especially as to the enemy's movements, good at asking questions, and thoroughly familiar with the terrain he is working in. Given that he is an armed fighter, he is unlikely to be able to carry on with his normal job for very long without being identified. It will be then that the job of 'expropriation' becomes necessary. In fact, it is impossible for an urban guerrilla to subsist or survive without taking part in the battle of expropriation.

In the context of the class struggle – which must, and will inevitably, become more intense – the urban guerrilla's armed struggle is directed to two objectives:

(1) The physical liquidation of the high- and low-ranking officers of both the armed forces and the police;

(2) The expropriation of arms or goods belonging to the government, the large capitalists, the *latifundiários* and the imperialists.

Small expropriations will provide for the urban guerrilla's personal livelihood; the larger ones will assist the revolution. But these two objectives do not exclude other, secondary ones.

One of the fundamental characteristics of the Brazilian revolution is that from the very first it has to engage in dispossessing the upper classes, the imperialists, the landowners, and all those rich and powerful businessmen involved in imports and exports.

The attacks on banks carried out in Brazil have done considerable damage to such capitalists as Moreira Salles, to the foreign companies who insure the banks, to imperialist firms, and to the federal and state governments – all of whose goods have been systematically 'expropriated'.

The gains from those expropriations go to the beginning and completing of the training of guerrillas, to the purchasing, manufacturing and transporting of arms and ammunition for the country districts, to the organizing of the revolutionaries' security network, to the day-to-day support of the fighters – especially those comrades who have been freed from prison by other armed groups, the wounded, and those wanted by the police or government troops.

The heavy burdens of the revolutionary war must be made to

fall on the shoulders of those who exploit and oppress the people. Those in the government, who are working for the dictatorship and imperialism, must pay with their lives for the crimes committed against the people of Brazil.

The number of violent actions carried out in Brazil is already high. They include executions, bomb explosions, the capture of arms, explosives and ammunition, 'expropriations' from banks, attacks on prisons, and so on – all of them measures which can leave no one in any doubt as to the intentions of the revolutionaries. The execution of the CIA spy Charles Chandler – an American officer who, having spent two years in Vietnam, came to infiltrate the student movement here – as well as those of several of our own secret police and military police prove that we have entered a state of revolutionary war, and that violence is inevitable. The urban guerrilla must therefore concentrate all his efforts on exterminating the agents of repression, and expropriation from those who exploit the people.

THE TECHNICAL TRAINING OF THE URBAN GUERRILLA

No one can become a guerrilla without undergoing a period of technical preparation. This involves everything from physical training to learning all kinds of professions and jobs – primarily manual skills. You can only acquire good physical resistance through training; you can only become a good fighter by learning the art of fighting. So the urban guerrilla must learn to fight in various different ways, some involving attack, others self-defence.

Apart from technical preparation, other useful forms of training seem to me to be hiking, camping, and spending long periods in rough country, mountain-climbing, swimming, canoeing, deep-sea diving and fishing (as practised by frogmen), fishing, shooting birds, and catching game both large and small.

It is important to know how to drive a car, pilot a plane,

handle both motor- and sailing-boats, to know something of mechanics, radio, telephones, and even electronics. It is equally important to know something of topography – to know how to locate one's position, to calculate distances, to make maps and plans, to measure time, transmit messages, use a compass, and so on.

A knowledge of chemistry, of colour-combinations, the ability to make rubber stamps and imitate other people's handwriting – these and other skills are part of the urban guerrilla's technical training. If he is to survive in the society he wants to destroy, he must be able to forge documents.

When it comes to medical care, obviously guerrillas who are doctors, nurses or pharmacists, and those with the equivalent skills, have a quite special role to play in prescribing and using medicines or performing surgery.

The most important element in technical training, however, remains that of handling such weapons as sub-machine guns, revolvers, automatics, mortars, bazookas, FAL guns and other types of carbine – as well as a knowledge of the various kinds of ammunition and explosives. Dynamite is one instance; it is vital to know how to use it, just as it is vital to know how to use incendiary bombs, smoke bombs, and so on. The guerrilla must also learn to make and repair weapons, to make Molotov cocktails, bombs and mines, and how to destroy bridges, dislodge or destroy railway lines and sleepers.

The urban guerrilla will complete his training in a specially organized technical centre, but only after being tested in action, having actually fought the enemy.

THE ARMS OF THE URBAN GUERRILLA

The urban guerrilla has weapons which are light, easy to replace, and usually either stolen from the enemy, bought or made on the spot. Light weapons can be handled and transported quickly. Their chief characteristic is being short-barrelled; they may include various automatic and semi-automatic arms which, though they add considerably to the guerrilla's fire-power, are hard to use accurately, and further, tend to involve some waste of ammunition except where the user is a superb shot.

Experience has shown us that the guerrilla's basic weapon is the sub-machine gun: it is effective and easy to hide, and is also healthily respected by the enemy. It is important to have a thorough knowledge of handling this widely used weapon.

The ideal sub-machine gun is the .45 INA. Others, of different calibres, are also useful, but are not so easy to get ammunition for. It is therefore to be hoped that the industrial logistic base will manage to produce a uniform type of sub-machine gun with standardized ammunition.

Each guerrilla group should have one sub-machine gun in the hands of a good shot. The others will have .38 revolvers, the weapon we all use. One can use a .32, but the .38 is preferable because of its greater impact.

Hand grenades and smoke bombs can also be considered to be light arms, useful both in defence and in covering retreats.

Long-barrelled guns are harder to transport and conceal. Among those available are the FAL, Mausers, shotguns and Winchesters. Shotguns can be useful at close range, more often possible at night. Airguns can be used to advantage for target-practice. Bazookas and mortars are also most useful, but only in the hands of well-trained men.

Home-made weapons can sometimes be just as effective as conventional ones, as in the case of sawn-off shotguns.

Comrades who are gunsmiths have a most vital part to play. They maintain and repair weapons, and may even be able to organize a workshop where they can make their own. Metal-workers, mechanics, and carpenters are all among those who should take on this work of industrial logistics; with what they know they can manufacture arms secretly at home. But we shall also set up courses on the art of making explosives, and on sabotage, with the object of trying new things out.

Molotov cocktails, petrol, devices for launching explosives, grenades contrived out of tubing and tins, mines, explosives made of dynamite and potassium chlorate, explosive gelatine, detonators – all these things must be in the arsenal of any guerrilla who is to be successful in his mission. The materials needed for making all these things must be bought, or stolen from the enemy by carefully planned and executed operations. The guerrilla must be careful not to keep anything that may cause an accident in his possession for too long, but try to use it at once.

The acquiring of modern arms, like every other innovation in the field, directly influences the tactics of urban guerrilla warfare. Once there is a standard sub-machine gun in general use, those tactics will be quite different. The guerrilla groups which manage to standardize their weapons and ammunition will be far the most effective, since their fire-power will be that much greater.

SHOOTING – THE BE-ALL AND END-ALL

The whole purpose of the urban guerrilla, his action and his survival, everything, depends on his marksmanship. It is indispensable for him to be a good shot. In conventional warfare, fighting is long-range, and the weapons are too. In guerrilla warfare, the reverse is true; unless he shoots first, he may be killed. And, since he will only have very little ammunition, and be part of a small group, he must waste no time, but shoot quickly.

Another point on which I cannot lay too much stress is that the guerrilla must not keep on shooting until his ammunition is gone: it may be possible that the enemy is not returning fire precisely because he is waiting for the guerrilla to use up his bullets, thus exposing himself to capture or death.

The fighter must keep moving as he shoots, or he will be a sitting target.

You can only become a good marksman by practising systematically, using any and every opportunity and means: target-shooting in amusement parks, for instance, or at home with an airgun. A good marksman can become a sniper, that is a guerrilla who can fight and carry out actions on his own. As such, he should be able to shoot well at long or close range, with arms appropriate to either.

'FIRING GROUPS'

Urban guerrillas should be organized into small groups, each one, known as a 'firing group', consisting of not more than four or five people. A minimum of two groups, working strictly separately but coordinated by one or two men, can become a 'firing team'. Within each group there must be complete trust. The one who shoots best and can handle a sub-machine gun will be the one who ensures the safety of the rest during their operations. Each group will plan and carry out its own operations, look after its weapons, and discuss and, when necessary, rectify the tactics used. The group acts on its own initiative, except when carrying out jobs decided on by the guerrilla 'high command'. To give free reign to this spirit of initiative, there must be the least possible rigidity within the organization; that is why the hierarchies which characterizes the traditional Left does not exist amongst us.

The kind of initiative that may suitably be left to the decision of each group will be such things as bank raids, kidnappings, the execution of notorious agents of the dictatorship, of reactionary forces or North American spies, and all forms of propaganda or wars of nerves. There is no need to consult the 'high command' before embarking on any of these operations. Nor should any group wait to act until it gets orders from higher up. Any citizen who wants to become a guerrilla has only to become an activist by his own decision, and will then be able to become part of our organization. In following this method, we make it harder for anyone to know who is responsible for this or that particular act; all that matters is that there should be more and more such acts.

The high command counts on these groups, and may send

them to carry out missions anywhere in the country, being ready to come to their help if they meet with trouble. Our revolutionary organization is made up of a vast and indestructible network of 'firing groups'. It works simply and practically: the general command gives the general directives, and those who belong to it act in concert – for anything other than direct action is not our concern.

LOGISTICS

Conventional logistics are expressed in terms of food, fuel, equipment and ammunition. But the urban guerrilla is not part of a regular army, and his organization is, and must be, fragmentary. He has no lorries or fixed bases, and it is very hard to provide him with industrial support. So we must express the logistics of urban guerrilla warfare in terms of Motorization, Money, Ammunition, Arms and Explosives.

Motorization is an absolutely essential factor in revolutionary logistics. We need drivers who, like other guerrillas, must be well trained. Really, any good guerrilla will also be a good driver.

If he has not the money to buy, then he must 'expropriate' whatever vehicles he may need. As with purchasing arms, ammunition and explosives, the guerrilla will steal the money from banks. Expropriations of this kind are vital in the early stages of organization. We must also steal the weapons that are for sale in shops, as well as those we find in the belts of soldiers of the civil guard, or the military. Later, when it comes to increasing our logistic strength, guerrillas will ambush the enemy to capture arms, ammunitions and means of transport. All these things must be hidden as soon as they are taken, even though the enemy may try to retaliate or pursue his assailants. It is therefore vital for our people to know the terrain extremely well, taking with them specially trained guides.

THE URBAN GUERRILLA'S TECHNIQUE

Broadly, what I mean by technique is the complex of means a man uses in carrying out a job. The guerrilla's technique – which he needs both for guerrilla fighting proper, and psychological warfare – is determined by five basic points:

(1) The special characteristics of this form of fighting;
(2) The advantages the urban guerrilla starts off with;
(3) The objectives he is aiming for;
(4) His methods of action;
(5) The methods needed for individual operations.

1. The Characteristics of Guerrilla Fighting

The technique used by the urban guerrilla will be marked by the following:

It is aggressive, or offensive. For a guerrilla, whose firepower is inferior to the enemy's, who cannot depend on powerful support, nor repel any large-scale attack, to be on the defensive is fatal. That is why he must never try to fortify or defend a fixed base, nor wait to attack until he is surrounded.

It is based on attack followed immediately by withdrawal – essential if the guerrilla forces are to survive.

It is directed to harassing, disheartening and confusing the enemy's forces in the towns, in order to make it easier to launch and establish the guerrilla fighting in the countryside which will be the decisive element in the revolutionary war.

2. The Guerrilla's Advantages over the Enemy

Urban guerrilla warfare is essentially directed to producing a violent confrontation between the fighter and the repressive forces of the dictatorship – the latter of course being infinitely greater. None the less, it is vital that the guerrilla be the one to attack first. The army and police will respond by mobilizing far larger forces, and the urban guerrilla can only escape pursuit and death if he makes the most of the advantages with which he starts off, which are the only compensation he has for his physical weakness. Those advantages are:

(*a*) Surprise in attacking the enemy;

(*b*)A better knowledge of the terrain than the enemy has;

(*c*) Greater mobility – or greater speed – than the forces of repression;

(*d*) A better information network than the enemy's;

(*e*) Showing such a capacity for decision as to encourage those with him, and enable them to act without hesitation at moments when the enemy is disconcerted.

(a) Surprise

Surprise is clearly a most important element and can do a lot to compensate for the guerrilla's inferiority when it comes to arms. The enemy has no weapon against it, but tends to become confused and simply to rush to his doom. In launching the guerrilla war in Brazil, great use was made of surprise, largely because of four basic facts we have learnt from experience which I may briefly define thus: first, we know the position of the enemy we intend to attack, usually because of precise information and close observation, whereas he has no idea he will be attacked, or where the attack will be coming from; second, we know just what the enemy's strength is, and he has no idea of ours; third, we are able to use our strength more economically and carefully than he does; and fourth, it is we who choose the time and place for the attack, how long it will last, and what we intend to gain by it – none of which he has any idea of.

(b) Knowledge of the Terrain

If the urban guerrilla wants to make the terrain itself his finest ally, he must know every inch of it thoroughly. Only then can he make the most intelligent use of its every detail – banks and ditches, irregularities, public roads and hidden pathways, derelict areas, etc. – in order to know how best to shoot, to withdraw and to hide.

Places where he could be cut off – dead-end streets, road-works, police check-points, military zones, tunnel entrances and exits, viaducts, crossroads manned by traffic police or any mechanical form of supervision – must be accurately identified, because a mistake could be fatal. What matters is to know every path a guerrilla can use, every place he can hide, leaving the enemy at the mercy of his own ignorance. With his detailed knowledge of the streets, and all their nooks and crannies, of the rougher ground, the sewers, the wooded ground, and any building work in progress, the urban guerrilla can easily elude the police, or surprise them in a trap or ambush. If he knows the ground well, then whether he goes on foot or bicycle, by car, jeep or lorry, he can always escape arrest.

If he is working within a small fighting group, he can easily arrange for them to meet again in an appointed spot before embarking on a further operation. It drives the police to distraction trying to find or counter-attack a guerrilla in a labyrinth of streets which only the man himself knows. Experience has taught us that the ideal is for an urban guerrilla to work in his own home town, since he will know that best; no one from outside, however competent he may be, can do the job so well.

(c) Mobility and Speed

The urban guerrilla must have more mobility and speed than the police and with this in mind he will make a point: first, of being motorized; second, of really knowing the terrain; third, of sabotaging or interfering with the enemy's communications or means of transport; and fourth, of possessing some form of light weapon.

When carrying out operations that take only a few minutes, and if he is making his getaway by motor vehicle, he will only be able to escape his pursuers if he has first carefully worked out his route. He should operate only in places far from the police supply bases, so that escape will be easier. He should also try to cut the enemy's communications, making the telephone lines his first target.

The forces of repression have all the most modern means of transport: the object must be to slow them up by making them cross the congested centres of town. But of course bottlenecks can also be harmful to us, so we must secure a favourable position for ourselves – this by means: first, of creating an artificial road-blockage or breakdown, which other members of the group will do, using cars with false number-plates; second, by obstructing the road with tree trunks, stones, false road signs, holes, or any other effective method they can think up; third, by laying home-made mines along the route the police will take, and setting fire to their vehicles with petrol or Molotov cocktails; and fourth, by shooting, especially to puncture the tyres of police cars.

The job of the urban guerrilla is to attack, and then get away; in doing so with light arms he can foil a powerful and heavily armed enemy. Without light arms, however, one cannot be very mobile.

Guerrillas can always be motorized if they are attacked by mounted police, and from inside their cars they can shoot their assailants with ease. The great disadvantage of horses is that they provide an additional target for the guerrilla.

Nor does the use of helicopters offer much in the way of advantage to the armed forces; it is difficult to fire from such a height, and impossible to land in the street; and if they fly low, they are easy targets for the guerrillas.

(d) Information

The government's chances of identifying and liquidating the guerrillas grow poorer as enemies of the dictatorship increase among the population at large. Such people will inform us about the activities of police and government agents, whereas they will not inform them about ours. In fact, they may try to

Handbook of Urban Guerrilla Warfare 77

confuse them by giving false information. In any case, the urban guerrilla has potentially far greater sources of information than have the police. Though the latter realize that the people are watching them, they are unaware who is on the side of the guerrillas, and to the extent that they behave with injustice and violence towards ordinary people, they present the guerrillas with more and more allies.

Even though we may get information from only a tiny fraction of the population, it is still a most valuable weapon. But this does not relieve us of the need to organize our own information services and intelligence network.

Accurate information given to a guerrilla means that accurate shots can be fired against the system.

To combat us more effectively, the enemy will try to get people to become informers, and will send spies to try to infiltrate our organization. Traitors and informers, the moment we discover them, must be denounced to everyone. The more unpopular the government becomes, the readier the people will be to have revenge on them. Meanwhile, guerrillas must act to get rid of them physically – which the people at large will certainly approve and which will also do much to cut down on infiltration and spying by the enemy. To complete this particular battle, we must organize our own counter-espionage.

By living among the people, listening to every kind of conversation, observing every kind of human relationship – though being careful to conceal his avid curiosity! – the guerrilla will round off his knowledge. He must know what may be going on in factories, in schools and universities, in the neighbourhoods where the fighters are living; he must know people's opinions and states of mind, where they travel to, what their business is like, whom they are meeting, everything that concerns them.

The urban guerrilla never moves without always having in mind the concern for some eventual plan of activity. There is no let-up in the life of a fighter; he must always be vigilant, always storing in his memory anything which might be useful, either now or in the future. He must read the newspapers carefully, and follow other communications media, asking questions everywhere, and continually reporting to his fellow guerrillas anything that comes to his notice; in this way we have a vast network of information which gives the urban guerrilla a distinct advantage.

(e) Decisiveness

A lack of decisiveness can nullify all the other advantages we have been discussing. If he is not sure of himself, the guerrilla risks failure, however carefully planned his action. This capacity for decision must be preserved to the end – otherwise an operation that has begun well may end by turning against him, since the enemy will take advantage of any panic, or even hesitation, on his part to destroy him.

There is no such thing as an easy operation. All must be carried out with the same care, by men carefully chosen for precisely this spirit of decisiveness. There will be opportunity during the training period to see whether or not candidates have it. During that time, those who come to meetings late, mistake people's identities or fail to find them, who forget something or other, who do not achieve certain elementary standards in their work, who show themselves indecisive and therefore possibly a danger to others in the struggle – such people should not be accepted. A man of decision will carry out a prepared plan with incredible determination, audacity and strength; but a single indecisive member may cause the loss of an entire group.

3. *Objectives*

In Brazil, the attacks launched by the urban guerrillas have the following objectives:

To shake the basis upon which both the State and the domination of North America depend. That basis consists of the Rio–São Paulo–Belo Horizonte triangle, a triangle whose base is the line from Rio to São Paulo. It is there that the country's vast industrial, financial, economic, political, cultural and military power is concentrated – in other words the centre of national decision.

To weaken the dictatorship's security system by forcing the enemy to mobilize his troops for the defence of that area without ever knowing when, where or how he will be attacked.

To attack from all directions, with a lot of small armed groups, wholly separated without even any liaison agents, so as to disperse the government forces. Rather than giving the dictatorship a chance to concentrate its apparatus of repression by confronting it with a compact army, we shall appear all over the country with our widely fragmented organization.

To prove our readiness to fight, our determination, our perseverance and our strength, so as to lead all who dislike the situation to follow our example and, like us, use the tactics of urban guerrilla warfare. If this happens, the dictatorship will have to send soldiers to guard banks, industries, gunsmiths' shops, barracks, prisons, administration buildings, radio and television stations, North American firms, gasometers, oil refineries, ships, planes, ports, airports, hospitals, embassies, food warehouses, the homes of ministers, generals and other leading figures in the régime, police headquarters, and so on.

Gradually to add to the disturbances by launching an endless series of unforeseeable operations, thus forcing the government to keep the majority of its troops in the towns and weakening their numbers in the country.

To force the army and the police, their commanding officers, senior and junior ranks, to leave the comfort and peace of their headquarters and routines, and keep them in a state of alert and permanent nervous tension, or lead them along false trails.

To avoid open combat and decisive battles, but stick to surprise lightning attacks.

To ensure the urban guerrilla great freedom of movement and action, so that he can keep up a sustained rhythm of violence himself, assist in launching rural guerrilla warfare, and later on, help to form the revolutionary army of national liberation.

4. *Methods of Action*

To achieve the above-named objectives, the urban guerrilla must make use of the most varied possible methods of action, but they must always be chosen with great care.

Some actions are straightforward, others more complex. The novice must ascend the scale, starting with the simple, and going on to the complicated. Before undertaking any mission, he must consider the means and personnel at his disposal, and count on the collaboration only of technically trained men. Having taken these precautions, he may consider the following possible methods of action:

(*a*) Attack;
(*b*) Entry or break-in;
(*c*) Occupation;
(*d*) Ambush;
(*e*) Tactical street fighting;
(*f*) Strike, or other interruption of work;
(*g*) Desertion, and appropriation or 'expropriation' of arms, ammunition and explosives;
(*h*) Liberating prisoners;
(*i*) Execution;
(*j*) Kidnapping;
(*k*) Sabotage;
(*l*) Terrorism;
(*m*) Armed propaganda;
(*n*) The war of nerves.

(a) Attacks

There are some raids that have to be carried out during the day, such as attacking a post office van; others at night, which is better for the guerrilla. Ideally, all attacks should take place at night, since that increases the value of surprise and also assists escape.

There is a difference between attacking stationary targets, such as banks, offices, barracks, prisons, radio stations, etc., and attacking moving targets, such as trains, lorries, cars, ships, planes, etc. If it seems too difficult to destroy such moving targets, it may be possible to stop them, by setting up road-blocks, for instance, or organizing ambushes.

Heavy vehicles, trains, ships in port, and planes can be attacked, and their drivers or pilots forced by the guerrillas to change direction.

Bank raids are the most popular form of action. In Brazil they are very common; we have almost made them a kind of entrance exam for apprenticeship in the technique of revolutionary war. Various methods may be adopted in such attacks: the staff of a bank can be locked in the toilets or made to sit on the ground, the soldiers guarding it immobilized and their weapons taken from them, while the manager is forced to open the strong-room. To confuse the police, one can use disguise, and when escaping, one should shoot at the tyres of the cars trying to give chase. Burglar alarms or other forms of police warning need not stop the guerrilla. He too will use new methods – more guns perhaps, or a larger group – and will plan every tiniest detail of the attack.

In this particular activity, revolutionaries have two types of competitors – bandits and right-wing counter-revolutionaries. This to some extent confuses the ordinary people, and therefore the guerrilla will try to make clear the political purpose of his action, in two ways: he will refuse to behave like a bandit, either by misguided violence, or by taking money or personal possessions from customers who may be in the bank; and he will back up his expropriation by some form of propaganda – writing slogans attacking the ruling classes and imperialism on the walls, handing out pamphlets, or giving people leaflets explaining the political purpose of what he is doing.

(b) Entries and Break-ins

Entries and break-ins are lightning attacks on buildings, on the edges of a town or even in the centre. Some entries will have a twofold object: to expropriate, carry out reprisals, set free imprisoned comrades, etc., and also to disorganize the enemy's supply system, and force him to move elsewhere, and draw him away from his bases.

Other entries may be made in order to get hold of documents or secret papers that give proof of corruption, of misuse of funds, of bribery, or of criminal transactions with the North Americans on the part of members of our government.

(c) Occupations

A group of urban guerrillas may attack a place, establish themselves there and resist the enemy for some time, for purposes of propaganda. Occupations of schools, factories and radio stations are especially valuable, as they have wide repercussions. But since they involve a greater danger of losing men and equipment, the withdrawal has to be well planned. In any case, the more rapidly the projected propaganda operation is carried out, the better.

(d) Ambushes

Ambushes are attacks that succeed by surprise. They consist in luring the enemy into a trap, for instance by issuing false appeals for help, and the object is either to kill the enemy, or take away his weapons. A single sniper can best organize ambushes, since being alone, he can hide easily – on roofs, inside some kinds of building, or in the countryside.

(e) Tactical Street-fighting

This is the means by which guerrillas hope to gain the participation of the mass of the people in their struggle against the enemy.

During 1968, Brazilian students succeeded in carrying out some fine tactical operations, getting thousands of demonstrators to move against the traffic in one-way streets, and catapulting stones and pieces of glass between the legs of the police horses. In addition, we can put up barricades, remove paving stones, and hurl bottles, bricks and other projectiles from the tops of blocks of flats or skyscrapers.

It is also important to be able to cope with enemy attack. When the police advance with their riot-shields, you have to divide into two groups, one attacking from the front and the other behind, the first withdrawing while the second throws missiles.

When the enemy forces send a group of soldiers or police to encircle one or more of our comrades, we in turn must send a larger group to encircle the encirclers. When the enemy surrounds a school, a factory, or any other place where people gather, urban guerrillas must not go there, nor allow themselves to be taken by surprise. Therefore, before entering such places, they must be careful first to study all possible exits, ways of breaking through the cordon, and the most valuable strategic points on the routes the police vehicles will have to take. They will then select their own strategic points from which to confront the enemy, and the routes to be taken by the police vehicles must be mined. Guerrillas must never organize any meeting, gathering or occupation in a place without good means of escape.

In this way the action of the urban guerrillas will work in with the movement of the whole population: it will be the guerrillas' job to surround, support and defend any popular demonstration. They must be prepared to fire on those who attack the demonstrators, burn their vehicles, capturing or shooting their occupants – especially secret police, and high-ranking police officers who try to get through unnoticed by using private cars with false number plates.

Theirs is also the job of helping to direct the demonstrators, and assisting their getaway; in this they must be helped by snipers, so as to get the best possible cover.

(f) Work Stoppages

Strikes are especially important to students and workers. Since they are one means of pressure open to the exploited which really disturb people, the enemy will try to prevent them, or put a stop to them, if need be by increasing his fire-power. He will try to hurt, arrest, or even kill the strikers.

When organizing strikes, therefore, the guerrillas must so act as to make it quite impossible to identify those who are responsible. They will prepare the ground with small groups only and in the utmost secrecy. They will have a supply of weapons, explosives, Molotov cocktails, and home-made bombs with which to deal with the enemy, and to be seriously effective, they should also have worked out a major sabotage plan to put into effect at the right moment.

Though they may be quite short, work stoppages and student strikes still worry the enemy considerably. For, in fact, it only requires the appearance of groups from unexpected directions to disturb the rhythm of daily life somewhere, and working in unpredictable ways, to cause immense agitation – which is in itself a guerrilla activity.

During such work stoppages, the guerrillas should be able to occupy the place concerned, capturing prisoners and taking hostages – especially those who are well-known enemy agents – who may be exchanged for imprisoned strikers.

Strikes can also assist in laying the ground for ambushes directed to the physical liquidation of the most bloodthirsty of the police, and those known to have tortured our comrades.

(g) Desertions, and the Removal or 'Expropriation' of Arms, Ammunition and Explosives

Arms can be taken from barracks, ships, military hospitals, etc. The urban guerrilla who happens to be a private, corporal, sergeant, or officer in the army, will desert *when the time is ripe*, taking with him as much as he can in the way of modern arms and ammunitions to be used in the service of the revolution.

One such 'ripe time' will be when a soldier is called to come out from his garrison and fight against his fellow guerrillas; that will give him an ideal opportunity to hand over to them his arms, and any vehicle he may be driving, or plane he is piloting.

There is great advantage in getting our supplies in this way; the guerrillas can be provided with arms and ammunition from government vehicles on the spot, and very little trouble is involved.

Comrades in the armed forces must, whatever happens, watch out for any chance they may get to help the revolutionaries in this way. If their commanding officers are slack, enmeshed in bureaucracy and not doing their job properly, they need take no measures to improve matters, but simply inform the revolutionary organization they belong to, and prepare to desert, either alone or with others, being careful to take as much with them as they can.

Incursions by guerrillas into barracks or other military buildings, carried out for the purpose of stealing arms, can be organized with the help of comrades in the army.

If there is really no possibility of their deserting and getting away with arms, then those comrades must turn their attention to sabotage: they can blow up or set fire to depôts where arms, ammunition and explosives are kept, and all such activities will considerably weaken and discourage the enemy.

Guerrillas can also capture weapons by grabbing them from sentries or anyone else performing a function of surveillance or repression. This may be done either violently, or subtly. When you disarm an enemy, you must always search him thoroughly to make sure he has not got another weapon hidden somewhere which he can then use against you.

The more patriots who decide to become activists, the more necessary such arms captures will become. The guerrilla will often start fighting with a weapon he has bought or stolen; he must then go on to act boldly and decisively, for we are only as strong as our weapons.

In attacks on banks, we must also systematically seize the

arms of the civil-guard soldiers on duty there, as well as any the managers or cashiers may have.

Finally, one can also get arms at the expense of police stations, gunsmiths' shops and arms factories, by organizing raids against them. Explosives can also be seized for future use.

(h) Liberating Prisoners

Some armed actions are undertaken for the purpose of setting free guerrillas who are behind bars. Every revolutionary runs the risk of being arrested some day, and condemned to long years of imprisonment. This does not mean the end of his career; prison experience can be enriching, and even in prison he can continue the fight.

First, he will try to get to know the place itself thoroughly, so as to be able to escape rapidly and easily when armed comrades come to release him. No prison, whether on an off-shore island, in a town or in the country, is totally impregnable if the revolutionaries have the weapons and the cunning they need.

Every guerrilla who is still free will try to get to know the enemy's penitentiaries where so many of his brothers-in-arms are suffering. The fate of everyone in prison depends on the work of the guerrillas, both those still at large and those in prison themselves.

The following operations are all ones that may prove effective:

Mutinies inside prisons, penitentiaries, prison islands or prison ships;
Attacks from outside;
Attacks on trains and vehicles carrying prisoners;
Ambushing soldiers or police escorting groups of prisoners.

(i) Execution

We should use the death penalty for such people as American spies, agents of the dictatorship, torturers, fascists in the government who have committed crimes against patriots or tried to capture them, police informers. Those who go of their own free will to the police to inform on our fighters, or who help in searching for them, must, if they fall into the hands of guerrillas, be killed forthwith.

Such executions must be carried out in secret, with the smallest possible number of guerrillas involved. Quite often a single sniper, patient and unknown, acting in complete secrecy and keeping calm, can do the job.

(j) Kidnapping

We can kidnap and hide policemen, North American spies, political figures, or notorious enemies who are a danger to the revolution. The kidnapped person will only be set free when the conditions demanded by the kidnappers have been fulfilled: the freeing of imprisoned revolutionaries, or the cessation of torture in government gaols.

To kidnap figures known for their artistic, sporting or other activities who have not expressed any political views may possibly provide a form of propaganda favourable to the revolutionaries, but should only be done in very special circumstances, and in such a way as to be sure people will accept it sympathetically.

Kidnapping American personalities who live in Brazil, or who have come to visit here, is a most important form of protest against the penetration of US imperialism into our country.

(k) Sabotage

The purpose of sabotage is to destroy, and it can be done by a very tiny group, or even a single man. When a guerrilla decides on sabotage, he will first act alone. Later on, he will act with others in such a way as to help make sabotage a common and accepted form of action by everyone.

Effective sabotage requires study, planning and perfect execution. The most characteristic kinds of sabotage are dynamiting, arson and mining. A few grains of sand, a tiny escape of fuel, inadequate lubrication, a pin not properly screwed in, a short circuit, poorly cut pieces of wood or metal – any of these may cause irreparable disaster.

Sabotage is used to weaken, render defective, or even wholly destroy such vital supports of the enemy's system as:

The economy of the country, with special reference to the whole network of commerce at home and abroad, and the sectors of foreign exchange, banking and revenue;

Agricultural and industrial production;

The transport and communications systems;

The work of repression by army and police, in particular their buildings and depôts;

The firms and goods of North Americans living here.

Those in the best position to carry out industrial sabotage are the workers, for they will know better than anyone the factories they are working in, and which machines have pieces whose loss could bring the whole production process to a halt.

When it comes to sabotaging means of transport, one must take great care not to cause the death of travellers, especially on suburban and long-distance trains, since they mainly carry working people. In any case the prime object is to destroy the communications services used for military purposes. To derail the carriages of a train carrying fuel touches the enemy at what is for him a most vital point. The same is true of dynamiting bridges and railways, for it may take months to repair such damage. Telegraph and telephone wires can be systematically cut, and their exchanges destroyed. Oil pipelines, fuel stocks, reserves of ammunition, arsenals, barracks, and all police and military means of transport must be systematically sabotaged.

There must be as many – if not more – acts of sabotage

against North American firms and goods as there are against those of our own government.

(l) Terrorism

By terrorism I mean the use of bomb attacks. These should be undertaken only by those who are technically proficient in using explosives, and completely level-headed in any crisis. Terrorism may also include destroying human lives, and setting fire to North American business establishments or certain plantations.

If the intention is to loot stocks of food, then it is important to make sure that the people benefit from it, especially at times or in places where there is great hunger or life is very expensive. In the work of revolutionary terrorism the guerrilla must always be adaptable.

(m) Armed Propaganda

The work of armed propaganda really means the sum total of the actions achieved by the urban guerrillas, especially those carried out by force of arms. Modern mass media, simply by announcing what the revolutionaries are doing, are important instruments of propaganda. However, their existence does not dispense fighters from setting up their own secret presses and having their own copying machines – stolen if they have not the money to buy them. For it is vital to publish and distribute to everyone underground papers, manifestos and pamphlets attacking the misdeeds of the régime, or encouraging disturbances. The existence of this kind of press will also help to rally a lot of people to our cause.

Comrades with inventive minds can design catapults for distributing such pamphlets and manifestos; they will also try to get taped revolutionary messages out on the transmitters of radio stations, and write slogans on walls and in places from which they will be hard to remove; and they will send letters containing threats or propaganda, and others explaining the purposes of our struggle to individuals who want to be in a position to impart them impressively to the people.

Since it will never be possible to get help from everyone, it might be useful to popularize this slogan: 'Let him who will do nothing for the revolution at least do nothing against it'.

(n) The War of Nerves

The war of nerves – or the psychological war – is a fighting technique based on the direct or indirect use of the mass media or the 'grapevine'. Its purpose is to demoralize the government. By it we can spread false, or contradictory, information by sowing anxiety, doubt and uncertainty among the agents of the régime. In psychological warfare the government is at a disadvantage, and therefore will censor the means of communication. Censorship of course has a boomerang effect, since it leads to unpopularity; it also demands unremitting vigilance, which wastes a lot of energy. The means for waging the war of nerves are these:

Telephone and letters. By these means one can inform the police of the position of imaginary time-bombs and plans for kidnapping or murdering people, which will oblige the forces of repression to become mobilized to no purpose, to waste a lot of time, and to start suspecting everyone and everything;

Letting false plans for attack fall into the hands of the police;

Spreading baseless rumours;

Systematically making the most of the corruption, errors and crimes of various people in power, thus making it necessary for them to justify themselves or deny rumours that have been spread by the very means of communication they have themselves censored. Also informing foreign embassies, the UN, the Apostolic Nunciature, the International Commission of Jurists, and the Human Rights Commission, and the associations founded to defend the freedom of the press, about the violence and torture being used by the agents of the dictatorship.

5. *The Methods to be Followed*

Any citizen who wants to become a guerrilla can only do so if he fully masters the methods to be used. Criminals often make serious mistakes which are their downfall. Patriots must therefore be careful to copy true revolutionary techniques, and not follow the methods used by criminals. It is the method used that makes it possible to know whether a given act is or is not the work of a guerrilla. The methods to be followed will include the use or application of these elements:

Careful inquiry and information service;
Observation to check whether the information received actually corresponds with the facts;
Exploration of the terrain;
Knowledge and timing of itineraries;
Planning;
Motorization;
Selection and renewal of personnel;
Selection based on marksmanship;
Rehearsal by simulation of any action planned;
Execution of the action;
Protection of those who execute it;
Withdrawal;
Removal and transport of the wounded, being careful not to use vehicles containing children (it is best to carry the wounded on foot by way of paths too narrow for the enemy's vehicles to enter);
Covering up tracks.

HELP FOR THE WOUNDED

During urban guerrilla operations, it can happen that someone falls victim to an accident, or is wounded by the police. If anyone in the 'firing group' has been trained in first aid, he will at once do what he can; in fact, with this in mind, first-aid courses must be organized for all our fighters. Guerrillas who are doctors, medical students, nurses and pharmacists all have a most important part to play – they could well produce small first-aid handbooks for their comrades. A wounded guerrilla must *never* be left where he has fallen.

When the group is preparing for an operation, they must make sure of having medical help available. They may, for instance, use a little mobile infirmary set up in a car, or establish a comrade with a first-aid kit in some spot near the scene of the operation. The ideal would be to have our own clinic, but that would be so expensive that it could only be contemplated if it were possible to expropriate the equipment needed. Meanwhile, we can of course make use of ordinary clinics, though we may have to force the doctors to tend our wounded at gunpoint. Should we need to buy blood or plasma from a 'blood bank', we must never give the address where the wounded are staying, nor that of those looking after them. In fact, those addresses should be known only to the tiny group involved in transporting and tending them.

All blood-stained clothes, bandages, handkerchiefs, etc., all medicines, and anything else used in nursing the wounded *must* be removed from any house they have stayed in.

THE SECURITY OF THE GUERRILLA

The urban guerrilla is in constant danger of being denounced to, or discovered by, the police. He must be prepared for this by doing everything possible to safeguard his hiding-place, his person and his comrades. In fact, our worst enemies are the spies who infiltrate our ranks. Any who are discovered must be punished by death, as also must deserters who inform the police of what they know. The best way to prevent such infiltration is to make our recruiting as rigorous and careful as we possibly can.

Fighters must not be allowed to know everything that is afoot, nor even the identity of all the others. Each should know only what he needs to carry out his mission. Ours is a bitter struggle: it is a class struggle and therefore a matter of life and death – for the two classes are wholly opposed to one another.

It can happen that a guerrilla is careless enough to reveal his address or some other equally vital secret to a class enemy. This is a total disaster. Notes on the margins of newspapers, papers left somewhere, visiting cards, letters, tickets – none of these things will be overlooked by the police. No one must use an address book, or papers with telephone numbers or names, or any information about people or places or plans. Meeting-places must be memorized. If anyone neglects these pre-cautions, he should be warned about it by the first comrade who finds out, and if he continues to neglect them, then the others must stop working with him.

The security measures to be taken will vary according to the movements of the enemy – which obviously means that we must be well informed about them, with smoothly functioning information services. Hence it is extremely useful to read the newspapers, and especially reports of any police activities.

A guerrilla who is arrested must say nothing that could damage the organization, causing the arrest of any other com-rades, or the discovery of any of the places where they keep arms and ammunition.

THE SEVEN DEADLY SINS OF THE URBAN GUERRILLA

Even though the urban guerrilla may rigorously follow all the security regulations, he can still make mistakes; no guerrilla is perfect, but one can do one's best to reduce the margin of error. Here are seven failings we must avoid:

Inexperience, which makes one underestimate the enemy's intelligence, or assume some tasks to be 'easy', thus leaving evidence which may be fatal. The same inexperience can also lead to *over*estimating the forces ranged against one. Then one's assurance, decisiveness and courage will suffer, and one will be too easily discouraged;

Boastfulness, which leads a man to publish his bold deeds to the world;

Over-valuing the urban struggle: those who are whole-heartedly absorbed in the excitement of guerrilla activity in the towns may give too little attention to launching guerrilla fighting in the countryside. They may come to think urban fighting is decisive, and devote all their organizing powers to that. Towns can be strategically encircled, and then we can only evade or break the cordon if there is guerrilla activity in the country as well. Without that we are always open to severe damage from the enemy;

Disproportion between our action and our available logistic infra-structure;

Precipitateness, when we lose patience, become over-excited, and move into action at the risk of heavy losses;

Temerity, which may cause us to attack the enemy just at the moment when he is at his most aggressive;

Improvisation.

POPULAR SUPPORT

The urban guerrilla will always try to act in the context of some purpose that is advantageous to other people, thus gaining their support. Wherever the government's ineptitude and corruption are most evident, the guerrilla must show that this is what he is fighting against. For instance one of the heaviest burdens laid on us by the present government is a very high taxation rate: therefore the guerrilla will set about attacking the dictatorship's fiscal system, and using all possible revolutionary violence to hamper its efficiency. He will do whatever he can against the officials, and institutions of the régime responsible for the increasing cost of living, against wealthy businessmen, both Brazilian and foreign, large landowners, and all those who are making huge profits out of low salaries, rising rents and the high cost of food.

The stress the guerrilla lays on acting to help ordinary people is the best way of obtaining their support. From the moment a large proportion of people begin to take his activities seriously, his success is assured. The government can only intensify its repression, thus making the life of its citizens harder than ever: homes will be broken into, police searches organized, innocent people arrested and communications broken; police terror will become the order of the day, and there will be more and more political murders – in short a massive political persecution. The population will refuse to collaborate with the authorities, so that the latter will find the only solution to their problems lies in having recourse to the actual physical liquidation of all their opponents. The political situation of the country will become a military situation, and the acts of violence, the mistakes and the various calamities that fall upon the people will be put down to 'errors' by government bodyguards. Once they see that, as a result of the development of the revolutionary war, the officers ruling the country are heading for disaster, then the eternal temporizers in the ruling class, the right-wing opportunists who want to keep the struggle a peaceful one, will be the government strong men to embark on a process of 're-democratization', reform of the constitution, etc. etc., so as to delude the masses and lessen the impact of the revolution. By that point, however, no one will see elections as anything but a farce – and they are a farce which the urban guerrilla must fight with redoubled violence and determination. In this way, we can prevent the reopening of Congress, and the reorganization of the parties – both the government party and the official opposition party, which depends wholly on the good pleasure of the dictatorship, and whose delegates are no more than puppets in the same Punch and Judy show.

This will be the way in which guerrillas will win the support of the masses, overthrow the dictatorship, and shake off the yoke of North America. Starting with the rebellion in the towns, we shall soon move on to launch the guerrilla war in the countryside, for which the urban struggle is a necessary preparation.

URBAN GUERRILLA WARFARE AS A TRAINING SCHOOL

Revolution is a social phenomenon depending on arms and money. There are plenty of both in the country – all we need is the men to get hold of them. The men we need must have two fundamental revolutionary qualities:

(a) Strong political motivation;
(b) Solid technical grounding.

We shall find plenty of these in the vast contingent of those who are against the military dictatorship and the imperialism of the United States. Almost every day more people come to join the urban guerrilla movements, which is why, each time the forces of reaction announce that they have got rid of a group of revolutionaries, the group rises again from its ashes. Our best trained men, who are most experienced both in urban and rural guerrilla activity, form the spinal column of the revolutionary war, and the basis of our national army of the future. This nucleus, whose members will have no dealings with the bureaucrats and opportunists of a cumbersome government apparatus, nor with the long-winded political speakers and signers of motions, has no hesitation in carrying out revolutionary actions. These men are armed with a basis of discipline, a long-term strategic and tactical perspective, and a knowledge of Marxist, Leninist and Castro–Guevarist theory as applied to the Brazilian situation as it actually is *now*.

From that group there will emerge men and women with the most superb political and military training, whose job it will be to construct the new Brazilian society after the victory of the revolution. These men and women will be chosen from among workers, students, intellectuals, revolutionary priests and churchmen, and the peasants who flow into the towns where they are lured by the need to find work, and who later return to the country politicized and trained. It will be through urban guerrilla activity that an armed alliance is formed among these different groups. The workers have a thorough knowledge of

the industrial sectors to be attacked in the towns; the peasants
have an instinctive knowledge of the land, as well as being
extremely astute, and they are very skilled at communicating
with the masses of the exploited. They will organize the bases
of support needed for the struggle in the countryside arranging
hiding-places for men, arms and ammunition, laying in stocks
of food from their cereal crops, tending the animals the guerrillas will need for food, training guides and organizing information networks.

The students, whose great quality is their keenness of in-
tellect, are well placed to undermine the taboos of pacifism and
opportunism, and will not take long to acquire adequate political, technical and military training. And since, when they have
been expelled from the colleges where they are studying, they
will not have a lot to do, they can devote themselves totally to
the revolution. Intellectuals have a fundamental part to play in
the battle against the despotism, social injustice and in-
humanity of the dictatorship. With the prestige that attaches
to them, and their skill in communicating, they can keep the
flame of the revolution alive. Indeed the participation of intellectuals and artists in urban guerrilla warfare is one of the
greatest advantages the Brazilian revolution possesses. The
support of ministers of various religious beliefs is extremely
important when it comes to communication with the mass of
the people, and this is especially true of workers, peasants and
the women of the country. Indeed some of our women who
have joined the urban guerrilla movement have proved themselves amazingly good and tenacious fighters, especially
during raids on banks and barracks, and when in prison.

Urban guerrilla warfare is a wonderful training school. All
guerrillas whether they be drivers, messengers, keen marks-
men, informers, propagandists or saboteurs, all struggle, suffer
and risk the same dangers. All are therefore subject to the
same tests before being selected to join our ranks.

CARLOS MARIGHELA
Action for National Liberation, June 1969

T–D

CHAPTER 8

On Rural
Guerrilla Warfare

Brazilian urban guerrilla warfare started from nothing, since we had no weapons, ammunition or money, and were obliged to obtain them by expropriations. Today the urban guerrilla movement is established throughout the country. Our activities began with the subversion of the triangle between Rio de Janeiro, São Paulo and Belo Horizonte, which is the basic area of bourgeois wealth and strength. Within this triangle Brazilian revolutionaries created their own terror, raided banks and barracks, executed spies, freed gaoled revolutionaries, encouraged desertions from the armed forces, captured arms, ammunition and explosives. The students carried out memorable mass demonstrations and used correct street guerrilla tactics. The clergy – or rather priests and members of various grades in hierarchies of every religious organization – intellectuals and Brazilian women demonstrated against the military dictators and North American imperialists. The result is that urban guerrilla and psychological warfare are proceeding successfully. The atmosphere in the urban area is one of social rebellion despite the weaknesses of our propaganda activities, especially our armed propaganda; and all revolutionaries see and understand that we must overcome our weaknesses in the urban area and have done with unnecessary and naïve arguments about the leadership, in order to achieve unity between the armed groups. This unity must be based on the strategic and tactical concept of a revolutionary popular government aimed at expelling the North Americans, expropriating their capital and their collaborators, destroying the *latifúndio*, and achieving the liberation and dignity of the Brazilian people through socialism.

The first stage of the guerrilla war is on its way to completion, which does not by any means imply a slowing of urban guerrilla and psychological war. As the first phase of the revolutionary war draws to its close, we must be ready in the urban area to take the impact of the rural guerrilla war and face much greater persecution by the fascist military dictators, who will use the tactic of encirclement and annihilation against us. We must devote much more care and time to the completion and consolidation of urban guerrilla organizations, and bring urban subversion to a peak, diversifying its activities and affording the enemy no breathing space. There are no time-limits and there is no need to rush anything. It is no use making great advances in arms and money supplies and rushing to get to the countryside first with a group of men to start the rural guerrilla war. If rural guerrilla war is not launched out of the urban guerrilla movement and with a proper coordination of urban and rural struggle, the rural guerrilla movement will not survive. When we say that this year will be the year of rural guerrilla action we do so with good reason, because subversion in the urban areas has reached a certain level and the dictatorship is baffled by left-wing terrorism and the number of armed expropriations.

The second phase of the guerrilla war is rural guerrilla action. This is not a haphazard affair. It is the fruit of previous preparation and activity carried out in line with the overall strategy and tactic of the revolution. Without a strategic and tactical plan it is impossible to move on to the second phase of the revolutionary war and launch rural guerrilla war. According to this plan revolutionaries must have been working in the rural area before it is launched, and must have intensified efforts to construct a guerrilla support organization. We must continually go over the focal points of the guerrilla war, establish contacts, and imitate the methods used by Lampião to construct a network of peasant supporters who will give us shelter and also help build our information network. The Brazilian rural guerrilla war will be organized for movement, for mobile operations of every kind from the simplest to the most complex. A revolutionary war in Brazil will be a war of movement, as it already is in the cities. The Brazilian rural guerrilla war must develop out of an atmosphere of social rebellion in the countryside, just as urban guerrilla war arose from social rebellion in the cities.

Revolutionaries in the countryside must start immediately to expropriate from the *latifundiários*, just as we expropriate from the banks and bullion convoys in the cities. Landowners' plantations must be burnt; cattle belonging to the refrigerating plants, slaughterers and ranchers must be expropriated, killed and distributed among hungry peasants. The rest should be dispersed throughout the forests of Brazil to provide meat for the guerrilla fighters. The *grileiros* and North American landowners must be attacked and killed, as well as the estate-owners' agents and stooges. The same punishment should be given to foremen, administrators and bailiffs who persecute peasants and destroy their goods. *Latifundiários* who demand unpaid services from their workmen must be kidnapped and their goods expropriated. Truck shops and stores must be sacked. Private jails where estate-owners imprison their workmen must be destroyed. The same should be done with public jails holding peasants. Tax-office files should be burnt together with all documents, loan certificates and other papers relating to repayment of debts inflicted on the peasants. Where the *latifundiários* threaten to replace peasant plantations with grazing land, the grass must be destroyed. Forced evictions must be prevented. Vacant land and land divided up by estate-owners or big agricultural companies must be occupied.

In the second phase of revolutionary war we must create the same left-wing terror and the same anxiety for the ruling classes, military and imperialists as we generated in the cities. In this phase of the struggle the peasants must arm themselves at the *latifundiários*'s cost, taking from them all their arms and ammunition. As soon as social unrest in the rural area reaches a peak we will launch the guerrilla war. Then we will go on to form the Revolutionary National Liberation Army. Its nucleus will be the armed alliance of workers, peasants and students. The last phase of the guerrilla war will be a war of fronts and land manoeuvres.

The military dictatorship will be liquidated; the North Americans will be thrown out of the country; the people's revolutionary government will be installed; the bureau-cratic–military apparatus of the Brazilian state will be destroyed.

Broadcast from a captured
radio station, early 1969

CHAPTER 9

Guerrilla Tactics and Operations

The tactics of guerrilla warfare only came into operation within the Brazilian revolutionary movement when it had recovered from the surprise and bewilderment caused by the April coup of 1964. 1964 and 1965 were therefore years in which the movement was on the retreat. 1966 and 1967 were characterized by fierce ideological struggle within the organizations of the Left, and in this period occurred the deep split between supporters of armed struggle and rightist opportunists who preached a peaceful solution.

In mid 1967 the OLAS conference took place in Havana, and had profound repercussions for Brazil. Its decisions in favour of armed struggle won the support of large sections of the country's revolutionaries.

In 1968, thanks to ideological struggle and the impulse given by the OLAS conference, we went into battle. We were only a small section of the revolutionary movement. However we took revolutionary initiative into our own hands, alongside other forces, including mass groups especially characterized by the active and militant participation of the student movement.

1968 was a year of intense struggle against the dictatorship. It was a year of action specially marked by guerrilla operations and tactics, then being used for the first time by the Brazilian people against oppression. 1968 was, in fact, the year in which urban guerrilla warfare was launched.

We emerged from a period of plotting and conspiring and entered the revolutionary war, which we realized would be a long, slow war based on guerrilla operations and tactics.

We were in no hurry and had no deadlines to meet. Our objective is to wear down, demoralize and exhaust the 'gorillas' ' forces, bring them to desperation and finally topple the fascist dictatorship and conquer power.

How far will we get with this war? Will we achieve our aims?

THE DICTATORS' MILITARY SUPPORT

The military dictatorship has the country's armed forces on its side, together with the forces of the police and secret police. Both are repressive forces. The conflicts existing within these forces do not invalidate their repressive nature because they are only minor conflicts. In the armed forces the dictatorship finds its basic support, and this guarantees its power. Thus the dictatorship has large and powerful armed forces. Its firepower is infinitely superior to the revolutionaries'.

US IMPERIALISM: THE DICTATORSHIP'S INTERNAL AND EXTERNAL SUPPORT

Besides organized armed force and armed police, the dictatorship relies on the strength of US imperialism. This is due to the fact that ruling circles in the US have a willing instrument for their imperialist policies in the Brazilian régime. A special feature of North American support for Brazilian reactionaries are the loans made by the United States which further impoverish our country, with the added drawback that our mineral wealth continues to be transferred to the US.

The Brazilian military in power serve US interests. They are ideologically identified with US imperialism and follow the United States line in international affairs; hence their surrender of Amazonia to the US and the fact that they have no misgivings about the economic, political and military occupation of Brazil by the US which is, in fact, already a reality. It is an illusion to think these Brazilian military men are likely to rebel against the United States, since its government and monopolies maintain the Brazilian reactionaries' military machine. The Brazilian military dictators are North American agents in Latin America, and have made the Brazilian government into a spearhead against the interests of the peoples of Latin America.

THE BRAZILIAN OLIGARCHY'S SUPPORT OF THE DICTATORS

Brazilian capitalists and *latifundiários* also support the dictatorship. They form an oligarchy based on an identity of interests between the two groups most responsible for the exploitation, misery and oppression of the Brazilian people. Today the big Brazilian capitalists are associated with North American capitalism, and the remaining few who are still unassociated are rapidly becoming so. As far as the *latifúndios* are concerned, the biggest belong to North Americans.

The big capitalists and *latifundiários* have privileges to defend, and besides being associated with the US, they are obedient to its commands. This can be explained by the capitalists' and *latifundiários*'s fear of popular revolution. The triumph of the popular revolution would mean a radical transformation of Brazilian social and economic structures. The extreme measures taken by the big capitalists and *latifundiários* took the form of a deliberate agreement to transfer power to the military in exchange for protection of ruling-class interests.

THE MILITARY

When they took power with the April coup of 1964, the military dissolved the existing bourgeois order and replaced it with something more iniquitous and more brutally hostile in the face of popular discontent. Once they had dissolved the old order they established a military–fascist régime which is still bourgeois in character, but represents crude dictatorship by the Brazilian ruling classes under military protection.

The new military–fascist order is the fruit of a permanent political crisis which has been plaguing the country since the end of the Second World War, and has been a consequence of a worsening crisis of economic structures and the general crisis of capitalism of which our structural crisis is an aspect.

Military rule in Brazil has the following characteristics:

(1) The Brazilian state has been transformed into a bureaucratic–military machine of a blatantly repressive nature. The armed forces have been transformed into a police force for internal repression, and continue to prepare themselves for counter-guerrilla campaigns rather than for the defence of national sovereignty. Police, jails and courts have become military dependencies, and the military use them to maintain their control. The state has also become a financial machine for collecting taxes designed to finance their immense security organizations.

(2) Economic decisions have become the prerogative of the military and, through them, of the United States. The state monopolies were affected and are in the process of being abolished. State concerns are handed over to the military or worked by the military with foreign capital.

(3) Political decisions have been put in military hands and the highest post in the executive has been reserved for one of their men. Parliament and political parties obey military instructions and are punished for failure to do so.

(4) Main government posts are occupied by members of the military or by men in their confidence who follow their instructions implicitly.

EMERGENCY DECREES (*ATOS INSTITUCIONAIS*)

Wishing to protect ruling-class interests, the military made the fascist coup and invested themselves with power by using the fire-power they have at their disposal. Immediately they promulgated the Institutional Acts or emergency decrees designed to legalize the extraordinary powers they had in reality already acquired through the armed coup. These decrees are designed to further their campaign of repressing the people and revolutionaries by destroying all freedoms, while permitting an attack on bourgeois liberal institutions and older politicians who have stood in the way of the dictatorship. The most recent example of the powers taken by the military is Institutional Act No. 5. By creating a coup within the coup on 13 December 1968, the military went much further than April 1964 and decreed the closing of parliament and stiffer press censorship; they jailed suspects indiscriminately, entered homes, killed and ill-treated detainees, deported them to concentration camps, suspended court protection and suppressed political rights.

Institutional Act No. 5 is yet another act of violence against the masses' protests at the iniquity of the country's obsolete economic structure. It also signifies an open attack on the older politicians who were attempting opposition to some dictatorship policies. The dictatorship justified the act by saying it was in response to the following factors:

(*a*) A flare-up of political crisis in the country and 'collapse of political power';

(*b*) The need to prevent the country being dragged into 'irremediable disorder and civil war'.

Thus the dictatorship was forced to admit that in four years of extraordinary power it had failed to check the advance of the revolutionary movement, and had failed to organize a stable political régime which could survive the political crises periodically affecting the country. By this confession the dictatorship showed it was ready to follow an iron-handed policy and to destroy all hopes of a political solution through an amnesty, direct elections and so-called 'redemocratization'.

THE REVOLUTIONARIES' OBJECTIVES

The objective of the Brazilian revolutionaries is to subvert the present military–fascist régime and ultimately to overthrow the dictatorship. For the revolutionaries subversion of the existing order is necessary and legitimate, since the existing order is evil and designed to defend the interests of capitalists, *latifundiários* and North American imperialism. We must destroy the order established by enemies of our country.

The first step towards this is to subvert the military dictatorship which represents the ruling classes. To overthrow them is to overthrow Brazilian capitalism, the *latifúndio* and US imperialism.

The revolutionaries' objectives are one thing; the bourgeois opposition's objectives are another. The bourgeois opposition arose out of conflicts between civil and military authorities which were produced by the expansion of the coup and the promulgation of the emergency decrees by the military. As far as the bourgeoisie is concerned, 'civil rule' means the rule of former members of the executive, judiciary and legislature who came from the civilian élite of the ruling classes and not from the military. This élite was ousted and replaced by the military, but hopes to regain power.

The revolutionaries' struggle has nothing to do with replacing military by civilian rule. We are seeking a radical transformation of present-day Brazilian society and we aim to replace the ruling classes, not simply to change individuals within it. We aim to destroy the power of the ruling classes. Our struggle is to overthrow the military and fascist state apparatus of the coup and the wealthy capitalists and *latifundiários* who are in the pay of North American capitalism, and to replace them by the armed people.

FORCES SUPPORTING THE REVOLUTION

The revolutionaries cannot achieve their objectives without the backing of the classes capable of struggling to take power. In Brazil these classes are the proletariat, peasantry and middle classes. Thanks to their patriotic motivation and attitude towards socialism and national liberation, they are the class enemies of capitalism, the *latifúndio* and US imperialism.

The proletariat is the only class interested in socialism at the moment; but all classes which oppose the ruling classes are united in their rejection of US imperialism and in their support for national liberation. Both in rural and urban areas the revolutionaries count on the support of these classes to launch the struggle against the dictatorship and US imperialism. When urban guerrilla warfare was initiated in 1968 and guerrilla activities began to proliferate throughout the country, these were in fact the classes which supported the new movement to a greater or lesser degree. Guerrillas continue to count on the support of such elements to pursue their armed struggle and take power.

REVOLUTIONARY WAR AND FIRE-POWER

The revolutionaries will achieve their objectives by organizing for revolutionary war. Revolutionary war is the people's best way of organizing violence in reply to the violence used by the enemy. Revolutionary war is planned war organized from below; and it is prolonged war because we are not interested in decisive battles, since we aim to exhaust the enemy slowly. This means that we must continue revolutionary war until the enemy can fight no longer due to the collapse of his fire-power.

Revolutionary war appears in concrete form with the emergence of urban and rural guerrilla warfare, and develops from guerrilla tactics to open manoeuvres. The emergence of guerrilla warfare in Brazil in 1968 signified a change in the content and form of our combat techniques which took us out of a situation dominated by mass-struggle techniques, like demonstrations and strikes, into one characterized by armed operations with small groups.

Change from one type of organization to another does not mean the exclusion of either of them. On the contrary, experience shows that mass-struggle techniques work in combination with the activities of small armed groups. But they are in an inferior position when faced with the systematic use of firearms by the reactionaries against unarmed crowds, and by organizing in armed groups the revolutionaries were able to compensate the inferiority of mass-struggle techniques. Now we are equipped with our own fire-power, which allows us to face the dictatorship and its repressive military forces, and to adopt a revolutionary strategy using military tactics. This is why the technique of small armed groups has predominated over all others. This change in the Brazilian revolutionary movement was due to the revolutionaries' decision to use revolutionary fire-power.

THE MILITARY BLOCKADE AND URBAN GUERRILLA WARFARE

As a positive form of action within the revolutionary movement, urban guerrilla warfare represents a daring initiative and innovation on the revolutionaries' part. Guerrilla techniques are to be used in the situation of blockade and strategic encirclement which has been established by the military. The enemy has blockaded the urban areas along the coasts where population is densest due to the pattern of colonization in Brazil. The reactionary military forces deployed along the coast claim to be safeguarding national sovereignty; but their real intention is to prevent any popular revolt against the ruling classes. By launching guerrilla warfare in the coastal area, the revolutionaries are in fact initiating the struggle in a blockade situation and they cannot therefore expect that their operations will break the blockade.

What we can aim at with this kind of struggle is a tactical objective, i.e. to distract the enemy's military forces, inflict loss on them and make it difficult for them to concentrate their firepower and forces in the campaign against the rural guerrillas. It is also possible that under harassment from guerrilla operations the enemy will try to increase its police forces and go on to use the army, navy and air force for punitive expeditions and manhunts. This will increase the dictatorship's costs to an excessive degree, and cause it more problems and growing disappointment when it discovers the impossibility of halting guerrilla operations by an opponent who leaves no trails and refuses to fight in the open.

CONTENT AND FORM OF THE ARMED STRUGGLE

The armed guerrilla operations are at present fundamentally urban in nature and organized in response to conditions in the large Brazilian cities. They are operations directed against the interests of big national and foreign banks, North American imperialism and its Brazilian holdings, against CIA spies and the property of the federal government and the United States, and against the repressive apparatus of the military forces. As far as *latifúndio* interests are concerned, it is the business of rural guerrillas to attack and damage them and create panic among the big Brazilian and foreign property-owners.

In the urban area during 1968 we dealt a hard blow against ruling-class interests in Brazil. In pursuing the policy of acquiring material supplies for the revolution and striking at the ruling classes and reactionaries, armed activities in our country took the form of expropriations, sabotage, revolutionary terrorism, arms raids, capture of dynamite and other explosives, armed take-overs, and capture of police hostages in exchange for political prisoners.

EXPROPRIATIONS

'Expropriations' are armed operations designed to acquire supplies and finances for the revolution. Many of the activities of small armed groups in 1968 involved this kind of operation.

One of the characteristic features of the Brazilian revolution is that it has been following a policy of expropriating from the ruling class and imperialists, and showing them what its future activities will be when it has finally triumphed and established a popular revolutionary government.

With expropriations carried out before the victory of the revolution, we wish to demonstrate that we will eventually expel the North Americans from the country and confiscate their property, including their holdings, banks and landed property. We will confiscate Brazilian private capital which has helped the North Americans and opposed the revolution. We shall confiscate the *latifúndios* and end the monopoly of the land. We shall confiscate the fortunes acquired by exploiters of the people. By using expropriations the revolutionaries are in fact applying the collection of the ICR or Compulsory Revolutionary Tax in response to the Merchandise Marketing Tax (ICM) levied by the dictatorship. ICR returns are devoted to the cause of Brazilian liberation, while ICM funds – besides being an act of pillage – go towards supporting the military dictatorship which is oppressing our country. Powerful Brazilian and foreign bankers, industrialists, businessmen and landowners must contribute to ICR or suffer expropriation by revolutionaries, as is being done now.

Revolutionaries – and outsiders – have been conducting large- and small-scale expropriation operations. As a form of armed struggle this kind of operation is inevitably similar to banditry, but the fundamental difference is that revolutionaries never expropriate from workers and the common people, never attack their interests or cause them any harm. Moreover, we do not commit murders but simply take goods unjustly acquired by the ruling classes, and take arms from their guards.

Revolutionaries attack not the people but the dictatorship and imperialism, and thus count on popular sympathy. By allowing expropriations to seem like acts of banditry and by avoiding any kind of evidence likely to lead to their identification, Brazilian revolutionaries gained time and confused the reactionaries, leading them up false trails. Thanks to this device, the Brazilian revolution gained a year over the reactionaries and was able to prepare itself for new missions relatively undisturbed.

REVOLUTIONARY TERRORISM AND SABOTAGE

When we use revolutionary terrorism we know that such activities alone will not win us power. All acts of revolutionary terrorism, punishment of spies or sabotage are tactical operations designed to demoralize the authorities and North American imperialism, reduce its capacity for repression, break its communications system, and damage the government, supporter of *latifúndio* property.

Revolutionary terrorist acts and sabotage are not designed to kill members of the common people, or upset or intimidate them in any way. The tactic of revolutionary terrorism and sabotage must be used to combat the terrorism used by the dictatorship against the Brazilian people. The dictatorship uses terrorism against the people through organizations like the CCC and MAC.* It uses violence without compassion or mercy. It pursues and strikes down people in the streets, creates fear and insecurity, raids homes, uses incredible tortures in its dungeons, and shoots detainees and suspects in order to terrorize the country.

We shall reply to this terrorism of the dictatorship with our own revolutionary terrorism. And we shall also use it against the infiltration and occupation of Brazil, both clandestine and open, by the North Americans. We shall take the same stand

* 'Communist-Hunt Command' and 'Anti-Communist Militia', both right-wing terrorist organizations.

with the capitalists and *latifundiários* who back the dictatorship and are working with the North Americans or are in their pay. Revolutionaries who practise terrorism and sabotage must create their own support organization to carry out their programme effectively. They need facilities for manufacturing home-made sabotage devices, and must work in small isolated groups. Addresses, names, telephone numbers and route plans must never be written down. Plans must always be kept secret and only persons going on missions should know about matters relevant to their task.

Revolutionary terrorism's great weapon is initiative which guarantees its survival and continued activity. The more committed terrorists and revolutionaries devoted to anti-dictatorship terrorism and sabotage there are, the more military power will be worn down, the more time it will lose following false trails, and the more fear and tension it will suffer through not knowing where the next attack will be launched and what the next target will be.

RAIDS FOR ARMS, DYNAMITE AND OTHER EXPLOSIVES

These tactical operations are indispensable to create and develop revolutionary fire-power. Recent experience with guerrilla tactics in 1968 shows that arms and explosives raids helped us move from a situation where we had no arms and ammunition or money to buy them, to one where we finally acquired our own fire-power.

Arms and explosives raids must be silent operations unaccompanied by publicity and disturbances. The most important preparation in this kind of operation is the place where arms, ammunition or explosives are to be stored following large arms or supplies raids for the guerrilla forces. We should never create large arms dumps with the material concentrated in one place. The correct technique is to keep several small arms caches on a totally decentralized basis, and never allow their location to be known to everyone.

In the case of small arms raids the material obtained can be used for personal use or for arming and supplying small groups. It is crucial to know the right moment for carrying out arms or explosives raid. At the same time it must be remembered that this sort of operation needs a certain amount of fire-power. By buying, stealing or capturing a single personal fire-arm we are making an advance because the essence of revolutionary activity is to progress from simple operations to complex ones. Whether the operation is carried out by stealth or direct violence or both, revolutionaries should never act until they are sure of absolute success and thus unlikely to waste time or lives.

OCCUPATION OF BUILDINGS, ETC., AND CAPTURE OF POLICE

Urban and rural guerrilla forces are both extremely mobile, and cannot undertake to defend fixed positions and defined areas or territory. Occasionally, however, conditions arise which oblige us to defend a position, especially when we are involved in mass struggle and strikes, marches or demonstrations. In such cases we may be faced with the necessity of occupying places of work or study. Such operations must be carried out, but have a strictly tactical nature and are consequently temporary. Basically the question is to occupy the site and distract the reactionaries as long as possible. As soon as the occupying forces' supplies or facilities are exhausted they should abandon the position and retreat according to a programme carefully planned in advance. No take-over or occupation should be tried without a good stock of explosives and petrol bombs being available, or without adequate fire-power being at the occupiers' disposal.

An example of the sort of operation under discussion was the occupation of Sé Square, São Paulo, on 1 May 1968, when revolutionaries together with workers evicted the State Governor from the court-house and forced him to take refuge in the church with his police and followers.

During occupation missions there is always a possibility of capturing policemen as hostages against the release of political prisoners or to force the police to suspend their torturing activities in the jails. Police usually infiltrate themselves into the occupied zone and can be captured; but if not, they must be lured into a trap. Once captured, they must be held as hostages until the planned exchange or bargain is concluded. Hostages' fire-arms should be taken and not returned. The police hostages we took in 1968 demonstrate the effectiveness of this combat technique within the mass movement.

BASIC COMBAT TECHNIQUES

For revolutionaries the fundamental techniques to be used in actual combat are ambush and surprise. To hit the enemy by surprise is the fundamental revolutionary technique, since it is in line with the principle of economy of forces and preservation of numbers.

Any armed action, whether urban or rural, requires rigorous application of certain principles of which the following are most important:

Information and intelligence;
Observation and tailing;
Exploration and reconnaissance of terrain;
Route-planning and time-table for the mission;
Planning;
Selection of personnel and reliefs;
Selection of weapons;

REHEARSAL

Retreat;
Concealment;
Exchange of prisoners.

SOME TACTICAL PRINCIPLES

In their initial phases guerrilla operations are dispersed. During the initial period revolutionary forces are scattered throughout the country to destroy and disperse the reactionary forces. In the next phase the revolutionary forces must be concentrated to carry out large-scale manoeuvres.

We must never fight on a single front. This is why we carry out simultaneous tactical or strategic missions, or use one to relieve the other.

Guerrilla tactics are flexible and are never bound by rigid principles: guerrillas attack and then retire, harass and retreat, occupy and vacate.

When we carry out any guerrilla operation our aim is to attack the interests of the ruling classes, imperialism and dictatorship. Consequently we never attack workers or members of the people or damage their interests. We must only use violence against informers or other enemy agents.

When a revolutionary group goes into action other revolutionary groups must do likewise on their own initiative. Confronted with several groups, the enemy is confused and must disperse, and cannot tell where to concentrate his repressive forces.

When revolutionary struggle begins with the activities of small, scattered armed groups and is not the work of a united front, this means that conditions were not right for the formation of such a front. A united front is a necessity, but it is possible for revolutionaries only when there is active fire-power available in the country. The creation and strengthening of revolutionary fire-power and its continued activity create conditions for the unification of the forces involved in the armed struggle. The united front is the fruit of active fire-power.

Guerrilla warfare is learnt in practice and training for action is done through action itself. There is no human profession or activity which can be learnt simply through books or mock action rather than through actual experience.

Operations must progress from simple to complex.

Activity should never be restricted to a single type. When the enemy thinks we are limiting ourselves to one type of action, we change to another.

When the reaction thinks we are likely to stay in one place we appear in another.

When the enemy thinks we are far away we are near by. When he thinks we are near by we are far away.

When there is an open road we advance. When we meet an obstacle we go round it. When the obstacle is impassable we retreat, because we must never fight in open territory or we waste men and supplies and expose them to the enemy.

When the enemy is unready we surprise him; when he is alerted we leave him alone.

When the enemy is angry we keep quiet. When he grows quiet we attack.

Whenever we can beat the enemy with cunning and need not use our fire-power against him, we do so. Fire-power is kept for difficult moments.

Whenever we undertake a mission we take more fire-power with us than we need. This demonstrates the superiority of our fire-power and saves us using our weapons and wasting ammunition.

We should never let the enemy discover the revolutionaries' real strength. If the enemy does not know our real strength he has to imagine it and is in the dark; meanwhile we observe him carefully and only attack when we know we can hurt him.

The enemy must never know when, where or how we will attack next. If he discovers our plans or is alerted, we change plans completely.

We never challenge the enemy. When the enemy challenges us we play dead. We only return the challenge at the right moment when we are sure of our strength.

Whenever we have concluded a reasonable amount of activity or some major operation, our next move is to rest, review our position, and make new plans.

We never look for show-downs or conclusive battles. This is

why we always organize our retreat with great care. Retreat is more important than action.

We must never leave the slightest trail or evidence behind us, and if we should we work until we have eradicated the consequences of our mistake.

When we expropriate money we must never distribute it to the people, because this will give the masses the false idea that we can replace them in the struggle for power; and that the liberation of the exploited classes depends on the goodwill and enterprise of the revolutionaries alone. This would be a paternalist attitude, and would create false hopes among the people and discourage them from acting. Expropriated money must be used for arms, ammunition, training and other revolutionary ends.

When we have a reasonable stock of arms, dynamite, ammunition and vehicles we should never concentrate them in a single place but scatter them, using different places to avoid total loss in case of mishaps.

When we have fairly large armed groups at our disposal we should break them up into small squads and never deploy them all at once. We must avoid a situation where everyone knows everyone and everything in the movement. Each person should know only what concerns his work. The example to follow is Lampiao who, even when he had 150 men, always kept them in small groups and sent them on different missions.

We should never admit anyone into our organization without full knowledge of his past and revolutionary background. This is necessary to avoid infiltration of police spies.

Revolutionaries involved in armed activities know they are facing a dangerous enemy and that revolution is not a child's game. Therefore we never list names, addresses, telephone numbers, contacts, etc., and never keep maps, plans and itineraries. Revolutionaries work by memory.

Whenever we hold meetings we avoid gathering large numbers of people in one place. We are also careful to choose a place where we can use guerrilla tactics. If we are surprised by the enemy we must shoot back and carry out a pre-established plan to repulse their surprise attack. All members of the meeting must participate in this plan.

Whenever a large group of demonstrators, etc., is being held back by the police and a group of police moves into the crowd to chase someone, we try to surround the police with a still larger group of demonstrators. This tactic is designed to stop the police, to capture weapons and punish them, as well as helping the wanted person to escape.

Whenever a comrade fails to show up at a rendezvous we do not go to his house. He may have been arrested and police may be waiting at his house to ambush his friends.

Whenever we suffer losses of men and material we never retaliate impulsively out of an urge for revenge or to show our strength. We first try to regroup and tend our wounds. Then, and only then, do we try to attack.

Leadership among us is never based on appearances or personal sympathies. The leader is always the one who sets examples by action.

CHAPTER 10

Call to the Brazilian People

As supporters of revolutionary war we are devoting all our energies to the Brazilian struggle. The police accuse us of terrorism and banditry, but we are revolutionaries engaged in armed combat against the Brazilian dictatorship and North American imperialism. Our objectives are:

To overthrow the military dictatorship and eradicate the effects of its activities since 1964;

To form a popular revolutionary government;

To expel the North Americans from Brazil;

To expropriate the companies, goods and property of the imperialists and their collaborators;

To expropriate the *latifundiários*, abolish the *latifúndio* and improve the conditions of proletariat, peasantry and middle classes, at the same time ending tax and rent increases;

To abolish the censorship and introduce freedom of publication and assembly;

To free Brazil from subservience to United States foreign policy and guarantee the country's global status as an independent nation, at the same time restoring diplomatic relations with Cuba and other socialist countries.

In our struggle for the above objectives we receive no arms or money from abroad. Our arms are acquired inside Brazil, captured either from barracks or from the police, or given to us by deserters from the military forces, by such men, for example, as Captain Lamarca and the brave sergeants, corporals and privates who came with us when we retreated from Quitaúna barracks. We hope such actions will continue in future to frustrate and demoralize the 'gorillas' and strengthen the revolution. The money we acquire is public, and it is well known that armed revolutionaries attack the country's banks and expropriate from persons who have grown rich by brutally exploiting the Brazilian people.

The myth about gold from Moscow, Peking or Havana has ended. The bankers cannot complain. Last year they made profits of 400 billion old *cruzeiros*, while bank clerks earn pittances and have to wait twenty-five years to double their miserable starting salaries. As for the government, they have no right to protest either: a corrupt minister like Andreazza owns an apartment worth one billion old *cruzeiros* and gets commissions from foreign companies. The dictatorship accuses us of violence and murder, but omits to say who murdered Edson Souto, Marcos Antonio Brás de Carvalho, 'Escoteiro' Nelson José de Almeida, Sergeant João Lucas Alves, and so many other patriots. Nor does it mention who torture prisoners with electric shocks and the *pau-de-arara*,* and other horrors which would shame even the Nazis. The Brazilian military dictatorship uses means of repressing the people which are brutal and callous and designed to protect the interests of wealthy capitalists, *latifundiários* and North American imperialists. On the other hand the methods used by the revolutionaries against the dictators are legitimate and inspired by a spirit of patriotism. No honourable man can accept the shameful and monstrous régime set up by the military in Brazil. We shall reply with an eye for an eye and a tooth for a tooth. The fight is on. In one year of armed activity we have managed to inflict a hard blow on the enemy, who is now counting his losses and is obliged to admit the existence of a state of revolutionary war. In the course of their activities the armed groups have been expropriating Brazilian and foreign banks and have damaged the banking system in Brazil; they have expropriated from large companies, imperialist holdings and federal and state governments.

* Literally 'parrot-perch'. A torture in which the victim is hung from a stick and beaten.

Among our activities has been the heroic guerrilla operation to free Antonio Prestes and other comrades held in Lemos de Brito jail in the centre of Rio de Janeiro. We also executed the American army captain, Charles Chandler, who returned from Vietnam to spy for the CIA in Brazil – an action which demonstrates the revolutionary groups' concern to defend national sovereignty and interests. The anti-Rockefeller demonstrations in Brazil, especially in Rio de Janeiro, São Paulo and Brasília, where students played an outstanding part, also show that Brazil has repudiated the North Americans and that the latter's only support is the military régime. But the régime's policy of national betrayal is now too well known to be covered up or camouflaged by the 'gorillas'.

The revolutionary war in which we are engaged is a prolonged war which needs support from all sections of the population. It is a fierce struggle against North American imperialism and the Brazilian military dictatorship which is US imperialism's agent in the country. It is a continuation of the heroic struggle launched by Che Guevara in Bolivia. It is a far-reaching struggle aimed at transforming Brazilian society. Our popular liberation campaign is in no hurry and has no deadlines to keep. Nor is it a mere barrack-room coup or some such farce designed to change one group of rulers for another while keeping Brazilian class structures intact. This is why all the revolutionary groups in the struggle must carry on with urban guerrilla warfare as we have been doing, systematically attacking banks and barracks, expropriating, intensifying left-wing terrorism, applying revolutionary justice to enemies of the people, kidnapping and sabotaging, until we make conditions impossible for the government. We must attack simultaneously with as many different and independent armed groups as possible in order to disperse the enemy's repressive forces. We must gradually increase urban guerrilla disturbances through an endless series of surprise attacks so the government troops cannot abandon the urban areas without leaving the cities exposed. Such a situation will be disastrous for the military since it will allow revolutionaries to launch rural guerrilla war in combination with the irresistible expansion of the urban front. In order to assure mass participation in the revolutionary struggle our next step must be to begin the struggle in the countryside. This will be the year of the rural guerrilla war: the peasants' hour has arrived. Their cunning and knowledge of the terrain, together with their understanding of the exploited and humiliated classes in Brazil, will be tremendous weapons for the revolution. The objectives of this second stage of the revolutionary war must be to subvert the countryside, destroy the *latifúndios*, burn the *latifundiários*'s plantations, kill their cattle and use them to feed the hungry, occupy the land, liquidate the *grileiros* and the North Americans who use them to acquire estates, and to create the same terror in the interior as reigns among the military, imperialists and ruling classes in the cities. While continuing the urban guerrilla war revolutionaries must dedicate themselves heroically to launching the rural guerrilla war. Our efforts must be united to build and reinforce the armed alliance of peasants, workers and students, together with intellectuals, ecclesiastics and Brazilian women. This alliance is the great cornerstone of the rural struggle and rural guerrilla war, whence a popular liberation army will emerge.

Struggle for the unity of the Brazilian people!

Down with the military dictatorship!

North Americans out of Brazil!

CHAPTER 11

Letter to
Fidel Castro

Dear Comrade Fidel,

Now that the Conference of the Latin American Solidarity Organization is over, I want to write and tell you that I am in complete agreement with the resolutions adopted, and with your closing speech; and also to let you know that I have broken with the Central Committee of the Brazilian Communist Party. This I did in a letter from Havana.

As a Communist, which I shall always continue to be, I could not refuse the invitation from the organizing committee of the Conference. And I came to it not as a delegate, but as a guest.

I know that the Central Committee of the PCB is hostile to the OLAS and the Conference; they themselves made this public in their resolution of March of this year, in which they stated that they did not intend to be represented there. ... I believe that my own participation in the Conference in no way alters my position as a revolutionary; indeed I am honoured by the disapprobation of these opportunists, for it only proves that I have remained faithful to the Brazilian people's revolution.

My position in regard to the revolutionary movement is well known; I made it clear to the Executive Committee of the PCB in a letter dated 10 December 1966. It is curious to note that the Central Committee did not refer to my resignation, but some months later dismissed me from the Executive Committee on the grounds that I had missed three meetings. It is an odd kind of leadership that is so zealous in arranging bureaucratic meetings, and yet will not lift a finger to support revolutionary action or struggle! ...

I realized that genuine revolutionaries from all over Latin America would be meeting in Cuba, where they would discuss mutual problems, and lay the foundations of a global strategy from which they could then start to confront the global strategy of US imperialism ...

The situation in the PCB is that, since the armed insurrection of 1935, successive leaders have abandoned the path of revolution, and aligned themselves with the ideological and political ideas of the middle class. ... They have paid no attention to the role of the peasants in the revolution, but counted only on achieving success in the towns, and that by peaceful, political means. ... The Central Committee is afraid of the armed struggle, and wants to avoid having to lay down any principles for it by doing everything they can to hamper the actions of those who are convinced that it is the one and only solution ...

What we must do is intensify the ideological struggle, as was done here during the course of the OLAS conference, and move directly into revolutionary action. ... Marxism–Leninism must be unreservedly accepted, and must be applied in Brazil as it actually exists now. ... I believe that my break with the Central Committee will help to deepen the ideological struggle of the Brazilian revolutionary movement, and put a stop to all rightist and revisionist ideas.

The Central Committee promises to solve all problems during a 'forthcoming' – but constantly adjourned – congress, which, even if it does ever take place, will achieve nothing: the leadership has proved long since that they have no wish to change anything ...

The way I have opted for is that of guerrilla warfare, and we must set it on foot all over the countryside; only thus shall we fully become part of the Latin American revolution.

As I see it, guerrilla warfare is the only means of uniting all the revolutionaries in Brazil, and bringing the people there to power.

As a Communist, I am convinced that the step I have taken will have served, at least, to show what revolutionary behaviour can be like.

Proletarian greetings,

CARLOS MARIGHELA
Havana, 18 August 1967

CHAPTER 12

Declaration by the Communist Group of São Paulo*

With the present declaration we intend to publicize our views about the manner of conducting armed struggle in Brazil. This group consists of Communists in São Paulo who, because of their disagreement with the Party's peaceful policies, voted against the Central Committee and were expelled or otherwise sanctioned without being able to defend themselves, since they were not invited to attend the meetings in which their expulsion was decided.

The break between us and the Central Committee is definitive. This break was definitively confirmed at the time of the OLAS conference in Havana when the Central Committee censured us and applied extreme punitive measures against those who disagreed with their peaceful policies. These punitive measures were ratified and even stiffened in the course of the Sixth Party Congress, which was held without the presence of the members who disagreed with the peaceful policy followed by the Committee. Even the São Paulo delegates or their representatives were not given invitations to the Congress.

As far as armed struggle is concerned, we have already defined our position on several previous occasions, affirming always that we support non-peaceful means towards the revolution. As far as the OLAS is concerned, we approve and support the General Declaration issued by the conference and agree on the necessity of studying and following the twenty

* Issued at the time of Marighela's break with the C P.

basic points at the end of the above document. Our policies are those of the OLAS's General Declaration.

As far as guerrilla war is concerned, we hold the same views as the OLAS General Declaration which views guerrilla war as an embryonic form of the National Liberation Army, and as the most effective way of carrying out revolutionary struggle in the majority of Latin American countries. Consequently we do not envisage guerrilla war in terms of a *foco* – as our enemies claim. *Foco* tactics imply establishing a group of armed guer-rillas at some point in Brazil and waiting for other *focos* to emerge elsewhere in the country. If we were to follow this line we would be following typically spontaneist strategies, and this would be a fatal mistake.

For us the Brazilian guerrilla war has no hope of success save as a part of a total strategic and tactical programme. This means that guerrilla war needs preparation and that its in-itiation depends on this preparation. Preparation for guerrilla war is something complex and serious and cannot be treated lightly. Preparation for guerrilla war needs the training of com-batants, the acquisition of arms, choice of terrain, strategy and tactics, and also a logistics programme.

The logistics programme must be initiated now. It needs above all work in the urban area, since victory for the Braz-ilian guerrilla war is impossible without the support of the cities. On the other hand, the peasantry is the deciding factor in the Brazilian revolution, and the guerrilla war will never establish itself without work among the peasantry, and without being closely linked with them and firmly supported by them.

Finally, what we are hoping for is to construct the organ-izations necessary to launch and strengthen the guerrilla move-ment with an armed peasant–worker nucleus, with a view to transforming it into a revolutionary liberation army. For us the guerrilla movement is the vanguard of the revolution, and is the focal point of the efforts of Communists and other patriots.

For specific action like guerrilla warfare we need a specific organization, and this cannot be the old *Comité Estadual*.

* i.e. state as opposed to federal committee.

Therefore we consider that the former *Comitê Estadual* and its members and dependent organizations are obsolete. The intermediary committees, e.g. municipal and regional committees, the University Committee and other professional groups, are also obsolete since they form part of an obsolete organization.

The party structure underpinning the Central Committee and other groups was the creation of a system established by the Sixth Congress and was fundamentally opposed to revolutionary aims. The commissions, auxiliary sections (such as the union sections), are all organizational forms which give the party a top-heavy and inefficient pyramid structure. As a result they strengthened bureaucratic control, hindered revolutionary action and prevented the initiative of rank-and-file militants. Consequently they no longer have any usefulness.

The political professionalism of the old organization must also disappear, since one of its results was that the Central Committee corrupted many comrades, thanks to its economic power. The so-called party functionaries are always men liable to forfeit the CC's economic aid if they express opinions not shared by the party leaders. There must be professional revolutionaries, but their relations with the organization must be based on revolutionary criteria and must never simply be subservient to the leading group in power.

An organization like the old *CE* and its sub-groups is unsuitable for armed action and even less for guerrilla war. Our need now is for a small, well-structured, flexible, mobile and clandestine organization, a vanguard organization built for sustained daily revolutionary action and not for interminable arguments and meetings.

It must be a vigilant organization, severe with informers, which applies efficient security measures to avoid its destruction by the police and to prevent infiltration by the enemy.

Its members must be men and women who are committed to revolution. The Communists of this organization are comrades of both sexes with a spirit of initiative, free from all bureaucratic and routine preoccupations, who don't wait on com-

missars and don't wait for orders. No one is obliged to belong
to this organization. Those who accept it as it is and enter it do
so voluntarily because their only commitment is to the revolution. This organization will have a democratic revolutionary
structure in which action counts above all and the fundamental
concern is the revolution and individual initiative and enterprise. The organization will have three guiding principles: first,
that every revolutionary's duty is to make the revolution;
second, that we ask no one's permission to carry out revolutionary activities; third, that we are committed only to the
revolution.

This organization is now beginning to be formed by the
efforts of revolutionaries and without anyone's authorization
on the basis of dissident Communists and groups who oppose
the Central Committee and will not submit themselves to its
interference. Out of this rejection of the CC has grown a small
coordinating group dedicated to guerrilla activity, and groups
of revolutionaries.

We believe the time has come to have done with the endless
internal quarrels, and that we should not continue to waste our
time with struggle inside the CC. We do not aspire to creating
another Communist Party or any other party. What we want is
revolutionary action, preparation for and initiation of guerrilla
war. What we intend by our decision to *fight now* is to help to
free revolutionary energies which have hitherto been repressed
and to allow them to expand to their fullest.

WHAT ARE THE REVOLUTIONARY GROUPS?

The revolutionary groups form the basis of the revolutionary
struggle. Anyone who opts for armed struggle must realize he
will be facing increasingly savage persecution from the reactionaries and must be prepared for this. Large cumbersome
organizations are the death of revolutionary initiative, and this
was the danger faced by the old municipal committees and

organizations originating from the former structure of the party.

The revolutionary groups form the basis of the revolutionary organization. They are small groups composed of revolutionaries with the initiative and capacity to fight. The name these groups adopt has little importance. The main concern is to go into immediate revolutionary action.

All of us without exception must organize revolutionary groups or belong to them. The overall leadership of the organization belongs to the guerrilla movement itself, wherever it is. We are working for the guerrilla movement and all our efforts are at the service of the guerrilla movement.

Part II

CHAPTER 1

Political Essays, 1966

The texts in this section were written while Carlos Marighela was still a member of the Brazilian Communist Party. They are included in order to make clear how his thought developed from more traditional forms of left-wing theory.

A. Causes of the Defeat
and Present Outlook

The April the First coup came and triumphed without the anti-coup forces – Communists included – managing to plan any kind of resistance. The only organized mass resistance to the coup was the general strike, although this could not possibly succeed because of the general state of unreadiness.

It is worth recalling that when Quadros resigned in 1961 we were caught unprepared, and realized we were not ready to face up to the new situation. We saw then that new government crises would follow in due course, and that in the event we would have to act differently, doing all we could to overcome our lack of preparation. But when Goulart's government was overthrown by the April military coup none of these good intentions materialized. In other words we were still unready. The democratic process was halted in mid evolution and we went into a phase of reaction and retreat. The absence of any resistance was indissolubly linked with our unreadiness: political unreadiness and, above all, lack of ideological preparation; unreadiness amongst the Communists as well as amongst the whole area of anti-coup opinion. And all this became evident when we were faced with the April coup and its immediate aftermath, when without exception no responses or directives for action issued from any of the several leading anti-coup groups.

As far as the Communists were concerned, resistance was impossible because our policies had been developed, essentially, in subordination to the government's policies – i.e. in a condition of dependence on the leadership of the bourgeoisie, or rather of the section of the bourgeoisie then in power. This situation did much to destroy our authority and cancel our influence, both indispensable when it comes to playing a leading role in a united front, consolidating it, eliminating hesitant elements and adopting a clearly defined ideological posture *vis-à-vis* the most radical sections of the petty bourgeoisie. When proletarian leadership is subordinated to bourgeois leadership or identified with it, any application of revolutionary policies inevitably polarizes between Left and Right because the stabilizing ideological factor is lacking — the only factor that can prevent a loss of revolutionary direction.

The underestimate of the threat from the Right was the fruit of heel-dragging and false optimism on the government's part. It was imagined that the bourgeoisie would continue along the path of peaceful reforms under pressure from the mass movements, and that the Right would not revolt; and that if it did revolt the bourgeoisie would take the initiative in resistance against the rightist rebels. Time and again we repeated that a right-wing coup would mean civil war in the country, and that we would answer rightist violence with popular violence.

Since actions did not measure up to words in this respect, we must conclude that we were not ready. We were confident the government would resist. We didn't even bother with forcible condemnations of the coup. We omitted to alert the masses and failed to forewarn them for possible resistance. Lack of preparation and wrong class analysis are in fact the result of the leadership's neglecting to draw up Marxist tactics, and failing to take account of the principle of stategic withdrawal. Marxism-Leninism is totally opposed to the idea that the only thing that counts in the popular struggle is to advance. Consequently, when implementing the policies of support for bourgeois reforms it was not enough simply to point out the advantages for the masses. It became necessary at the same time to prepare and organize them for a possible reaction on the part of the bourgeoisie, or a capitulation to the Right or a military coup — always in the offing when the mass movement is growing to a point where it can threaten the power structure or make a break-through to a new type of democracy.

The increasingly obvious mistake, therefore, was an ideo-logical one, which can be interpreted as a loss on the part of the Brazilian people of a clear sense of the class basis of the revolutionary struggle. In the historical terms of our activity this mistake is obvious in the different and sometimes con-tradictory policies and tactics of the Communists throughout Brazilian political life. We can no longer postpone some de-scription of an obvious and long-standing ideological error among leaders of Brazilian Communism.

Lack of ideological grounding caused a potentially fruitful political line to come to grief. It gave rise too to the mistaken notion of 'a new strategy for imperialism', according to which North American imperialism is uninterested in coups and dic-tatorships. The April the First coup, inspired and fostered by US agents supported by their agents in Brazil and by the Braz-ilian military fascists, invalidated this thesis and left us be-wildered and unprepared when confronted with the fact of a right-wing coup.

A wrong assessment of the role of the armed forces deluded us as to the military set-up of the government, because the military was not influenced by proletarian politics and could inevitably never be mobilized in favour of the masses in any situation where the latter might threaten the privileges of the ruling classes.

Repeated calls for a political general strike, without peasant support or recourse to armed insurrection, amounted to an error in terms of contemporary Marxist thought. The error was all the more blatant because our work amongst the proletariat was taking on obvious characteristics of work done with the support and official sanction of the State. Another basic fault was the weakness of the peasant movement. A failure to decide to give priority to work in rural sectors is responsible for this fundamental weakness. If the peasantry is not mobilized the revolution is impossible. Neither did the Marxist leaders ap-preciate the genuine radicalization of certain sections of the petty bourgeoisie. And this, along with other mistakes, contributed to our failure to exercise any influence on seamen, NCOs and other radical elements, thus preventing any consolidated action with the united front of which we also formed part. Other factors which led to our defeat were mistaken directives, neglect of collective leadership and lack of ideological unity among the leaders.

Now we are confronted with a new situation. Instead of a bourgeois government fighting after its fashion for reforms within the context of certain formal freedoms, we have a military dictatorship selling out to foreign capital in a situation where democratic liberties have been suppressed. Our strategy cannot be the same as in the previous situation when the mass movement was in the ascendant. Now the democratic process has been interrupted and we are entering a reactionary period. Although the problems of Brazilian society still arise basically from the need for structural change, we can solve them only by overthrowing the dictatorship and bringing about the restoration of democratic freedom. Our basic tactical objective in order to achieve structural change and to advance the struggle for an ultimate victory for socialism lies now in substituting for the present government another which will guarantee formal freedoms and open the way for progress.

The government for which we are fighting can only be the product of a united anti-dictatorship front – the only type of united front possible at the moment. In striving to achieve this united front we continue to defend the need for an alliance between us and the national bourgeoisie, taking into account not only everything which links us with them as far as common objectives in defence of national interests are concerned, but also everything which separates us from them as regards class, tactics, methods, ideology and programme.

The form the main struggle must take now is that of mass resistance in its endless complexity. And the party must lead popular resistance lest we lag behind the bourgeois opposition, which is showing every sign of forging ahead and dragging us in its wake. We cannot abandon the struggle for the leadership of the popular opposition: this would be an unforgivable dere-

liction in the contest for a leading role in the destiny of the
Brazilian people. So we must be strong in the resistance
struggle, tireless in the battle against the dictatorship.

Many other tactical notions must be renewed in the new
situation. The mass movements – and we must go on fighting
for a change in their nature – can no longer aim in the current
circumstances at putting pressure on the government as if our
policy were to modify the dictatorship's politics and composition. The aim of the mass movement is to overthrow the
dictatorship and replace it by another government. The elections are also now different in character. Their objectives are
no longer what they were in the pre-coup period. It is not a
question – as it used to be when elections strengthened democratic freedoms – of electing nationalists and thereby working
for a change in the balance of power. We now need to strive to
consolidate the forces opposed to the dictatorship and to contribute towards its defeat by shrinking its social and political
base. If none of this is possible through such elections as the
dictators now permit, our duty is to declare the fact to the
people, although we must not refuse to use what limited legal
means now exist.

The party must cease to be a sort of appendix to the bourgeois parties if it is to take with it the people and proletarian
masses. If we stand beside candidates linked with the coup and
dictatorship, we lose status in the eyes of the masses and help
to justify the present electoral farce. What we cannot do is to
collaborate in the institutionalization of the dictatorship by
capitulating before its violence and threats, and allowing
ourselves to be fooled by its manoeuvres. For the dictatorship
the elections represent a means of institutionalizing the coup.
Direct elections have been suppressed and the people's right to
choose their own candidates has been limited. Some candidates
have been declared non-eligible; political parties have been
dissolved and other coercive measures taken. The elections
have become a farce. The powers of the elected delegates are
mere concessions of the dictators, and anyone winning an elec-
tion as an opposition candidate against them will be allowed

to act only under the direction of a military overlord appointed by the executive or the minister for war. With the autonomy of state and municipal authorities abolished, nomination for official posts is no longer the function of elected representatives, but is done by the National Intelligence Service or Council for National Security – the organizations through which the military powers work.

Firmly entrenched, with powers such as were never held by any previous Brazilian president – reminiscent of '*l'état c'est moi*' by which Louis XIV of France established absolute monarchy – the present president of the republic will try to guarantee himself a military successor through indirect ballot.

Despite the fact that the implacable actions of the dictatorship in crushing forcibly and methodically what legal means of expression remain to the opposition, the year 1966 is opening in an atmosphere charged with political tension due to the struggle for the presidential succession. There is no sign of an end to the instability of the political situation, itself a reflection of a deep structural crisis. Political instability continues to be characteristic of the country. The overall tendency is towards a sharpening of class conflict. Decree No. 2 and similar decrees show that the dictatorship cannot halt its headlong career towards disaster. Governmental crises, the possible emergence of a coup within the coup, a state of emergency, frontier conflicts and many other similar events – these are things closely observed by the Brazilian people.

Serious problems may arise from the disastrous economic and financial policies of the government, from unemployment, shortages, subservience to the IMF, anti-labour policies, and also from the policy of sell-out and surrender to the USA and from the growing mass struggle.

Another foreseeable factor in the Brazilian crisis is the aggressiveness of US imperialism, which is constantly increasing. The most recent example is the US House of Representatives' resolution for an American invasion of any country which the so-called Colossus of the North considers threatened by Communism; and here the word Communism is a bare substitute for the national people's liberation movements. If this example is not enough, one need only mention the invasions of Dominica and Vietnam. Brazilian troops are already participating in the Dominican invasion and helping, alongside the hated US marines, to massacre the brave Dominican people in their struggle for freedom. The contempt with which the peoples of Latin America view Brazil as a result of its servile endorsement of US imperialist aggression will certainly have repercussions among our people and inflame popular opposition to the Brazilian dictatorship.

Given some situation unfavourable to the Brazilian dictators, or their possible overthrow by the masses, it is not impossible that the US will come to their aid and the ruling classes' aid and carry out reprisals against the people and nation, and even occupy parts of our territory, for example the North-East. This would merely continue the economic, political and military aggression already under way in our country.

It would be unpardonable if the popular and national forces were again surprised by future events. For Brazilian revolutionaries there is no alternative but to prepare for combat.

B. The Brazilian Crisis and Revolutionary Strategy

The Brazilian crisis is a crisis of economic structures. In other words, the crisis in Brazil in all senses, whether political, economic or social, arises from the inadaptibility of the present economic structure of the country, from its inability to withstand the excessive demands made on it. Since by definition economic structure is the whole of the socio-economic relations within a society, we will find the causes of the Brazilian crisis in these relations and their problems. They include our property system, but not only that: they also include the men involved in the productive process as well as the ways wealth or material goods are distributed.

It is in fact these relations which are themselves in crisis because they are no longer able to provide the conditions demanded of them by our social and economic development, and represent an obstacle to our productive energies. All of this is evident in the domination of the Brazilian economy and property by North American imperialism, in the predominance of the *latifúndio* system of landownership, and in the unequal distribution of profits and fruits of labour which encourages the accumulation of wealth in the hands of a privileged few while millions of Brazilians vegetate in misery. Thus the socio-economic structures of the country present a picture of a system riddled with weak points which threaten to bring the whole economic structure crashing down.

The present superstructure of Brazilian society, which derives from the economic infrastructure and is underpinned by it, is suffering from many evils. The weaknesses in the economic infrastructure react constantly upon it, and it is shaken by crises and undermined by contradictions, antagonisms and conflicts. This explains, among other reasons, why Brazilian political institutions are in permanent crisis, and why political instability is typical of the Brazilian situation.

A curious feature of the Brazilian crisis is that it is chronic: since it is an aspect of the general crisis of capitalism, to every new phase of that crisis there corresponds a new period of economic crisis in Brazil.

Brazilian society has been through many important transformations in order to become what it is today. From slavery it evolved towards new types of economic relations – towards capitalism and a wage-earning economy, albeit still dependent on North American capitalism and with the land monopoly surviving with a strengthened *latifúndio*.

Nelson Werneck Sodré, a notable historian and famous literary critic, clearly understood the phenomena which conditioned the development of Brazilian society, and describes them in various works, including *The Historical Formation of Brazil*, *History of the Brazilian Bourgeoisie*, and *Military History of Brazil*, all works of great value.

Present-day Brazilian society is developing on distinctly bourgeois lines, but in its own and distinctly Brazilian way, thanks to the conditions which governed its evolution. The great structural changes which have brought it to its present stage of development originated primarily in the introduction of electrification. Unlike the great capitalist countries of today, Brazil reached a certain stage of capitalist development when the world had already entered the imperialist epoch and had divided between the two great social systems of socialism and imperialism. As a result, Brazil never managed to catch up with developed countries and remains, as everyone knows, an underdeveloped nation. And it must be stressed that it cannot follow the same course as other capitalist countries which achieved capitalism via an industrial revolution.

Brazil found itself on the threshold of industrial expansion at a moment when the industrial revolution had already been accomplished in the main countries of the world, and the contemporary period had acquired its fundamental characteristics. This explains why the Brazilian bourgeoisie never had strength or funds to establish basic industries in Brazil through private enterprise. To establish an industrial base it had to leave things to the State, which set up a steel industry, prospected for oil and expanded energy supplies. The State monopolies thus appear as a kind of national capitalism responding to the bourgeoisie's inability to create an industrial base through private enterprise.

The originality of Brazil's development does not lie solely in the fact that each new phase of industrial expansion in the country coincided with a new phase of the general crisis of capitalism. There is also the fact that each new step forward heralded new and deeper conflicts in the Brazilian social system which in turn inevitably implied a worsening of the economic crisis. Also, every new technical advance in the developed countries has its eventual influence – in a capitalist direction – on the productive forces of the underdeveloped countries. Some conquests of modern technology fail inevitably when transferred to Brazil, and this causes tensions and disturbances in the productive system with consequences for the whole economy and for the superstructure. Brazil is a country which, without ever managing to resolve the contradictions generated during the first phase of the general crisis of capitalism, is now obliged to face the grave new difficulties created by the two succeeding phases of the same crisis.

All of this gives us an impressive picture of the severity of the chronic Brazilian crisis, which has been generated by the growth of capital in a condition of dependence on foreign resources and by the survival of the *latifúndio*. Inevitably, the several social classes have sought solutions to this crisis, and with this we now move into the domain of politics understood as the ways in which the various classes attempt to gain power or solve their problems through state action.

The kinds of solution envisaged by the social classes of Brazil fall into two large categories, one corresponding to bourgeois and the other to proletarian interests. All solutions tried by the bourgeoisie bear the stamp of a class differentiated from the proletariat by its entrepreneurial character, possessing means of production which allow it to accumulate capital on an immense scale. The Brazilian bourgeoisie is also distinct from the proletariat in that it maintains very close relations with the *latifúndio* and with imperialism – despite its conflicts with the latter and despite the fact that the *latifúndio* limits its internal market. This is why its solutions vary between violence and suppression of liberties on the one hand to attempted reforms to a greater or less degree on the other. The period of Joao Goulart's government was one where a section of the bourgeoisie went farthest in the fight for reforms. Its inevitable failure was the result of the bourgeoisie's own limitations: the Brazilian bourgeoisie is characterized by its penchant for compromise and surrender, both a logical consequence of its situation and its ties with imperialism and the *latifúndio*.

As a consequence of the solutions formulated by the bourgeoisie – and as a solution in itself – the most the bourgeoisie of Brazil managed to give the country was a certain economic development. Although dependent on imperialism, this development signified a move forward, a real progress. But the laws of capitalist accumulation immediately applied, and it involved sacrifice, poverty and exploitation, especially on the part of the rural masses. The balance of the solutions tried by the Brazilian bourgeoisie – including the solution of capitalist progress – demonstrates their non-popular content, their generally anti-democratic direction and, usually, their collapse before the combined forces of imperialism, *latifúndio* and military coup.

In the process of applying its solutions the bourgeoisie has shown itself incapable of managing the political processes of Brazil either through failing to free the country from North American imperialism or through its inability to liquididate the *latifúndio* and the contradictions generated in the country during these first three phases of the general crisis of capitalism. There is moreover an outstanding feature worth noting in

Brazilian politics. Whenever there has been any move forwards, any conquest of social rights or move against imperialism or the *latifúndio*, this has been due to the active participation of the proletariat.

The traditional alliance between bourgeoisie and proletariat has been a constant source of contradiction and error in political life which has inevitably excluded the peasantry from participation in national politics. The group with the vocation, historical mission and conditions for resolving the Brazilian political crisis is the proletariat with its allies in the united front. By attracting the peasantry – the natural ally of the proletariat – into the struggle, broadening the united front and increasing its influence; by initiating confrontation, eradicating the lukewarm elements in the bourgeoisie (although maintaining its alliance with them at the present historical stage) the Brazilian proletariat has in its power the means and conditions necessary for the break-through our people need. Only thus will the combination of nationalism and democracy have the right perspectives and dimensions to adapt itself to the needs of the Brazilian people. Only by struggling with the bourgeoisie for national hegemony will our proletariat achieve this perspective.

The Brazilian proletariat has already formulated for itself one of the solutions to our chronic crisis by sharing in the process of national evolutionary development – having tried the revolutionary path in the ANL (National Alliance for Liberation) in 1935. That this has happened is due to the nature of our own proletariat since its origins and emergence as a class up to its transformation into an independent social class. The details of this process and the conditions which led to the formation of the proletarian vanguard thanks to a dramatic rise in its level of consciousness, are the subject of a brilliant study by Astrojildo Pereira in his *Historical Formation of the Brazilian Communist Party* – study of which is indispensable.

In France, England, Germany, Italy, the USA and other important countries the proletariat emerged as an autonomous

class parallel with the industrial revolution and basic industrialization which typify the modern era. The Brazilian proletariat emerged only much later from an elementary
industrialization which dated from the period of the Second
World War. It was precisely due to these circumstances that
patriotic slogans and nationalist, anti-imperialist, liberal and
democratic slogans reached a peak of intensity and popularity
throughout the country. The Brazilian proletariat grew apace
with the basic industries created by the State monopolies in
steel, oil, minerals and electricity; and it supported State industrialization, opposed fascism, favoured sending the Brazilian
Expeditionary Force to Europe; it supported the Constitution,
democracy and democratic liberties, resisted rightist coups, opposed sending troops to Korea and favoured peace against
war.

It was under the aegis of nationalist–democratic policies
that the Brazilian bourgeoisie managed to play a political role
while its expansion speeded up with the productive forces. On
the political and economic plane the evolution of Brazil and its
economic expansion were conducted by a section of the bourgeoisie – basically the industrial bourgeoisie. For the Communists – as for the Left in general – this meant a long period of
collaboration with the bourgeois forces. The need for the
struggle against imperialism and the necessity of fighting the
forces of the rightist coup who oppose progress and freedom,
put the popular and national forces and their revolutionary
leadership in a position of dependence on the Brazilian bourgeoisie. The opposite could have happened, but that would
have required a correct application of Marxism-Leninism to
Brazilian reality; and this did not occur.

Historical conditions and circumstances peculiar to Brazil
facilitated the hegemony of the bourgeoisie in the political
process. But the hegemony of the bourgeoisie is not a historical
inevitability, and there is nothing to indicate that the proletariat is obliged to adopt a conformist position and subject
itself indefinitely to bourgeois leadership. This subjection came
about, as we saw, because the revolutionary leadership has

limited its activities up to now to collaborating in the bourgeois–proletariat alliance which has been, in our history, a
consequence of the alliance of nationalism and democracy.

As long as the Marxist leadership limits its revolutionary
anti-imperialist and democratic policies to working for unity
and rivalry with the bourgeoisie, and merely maintains the two
classes in a state of alliance and confrontation, it is unlikely
that there will be a revolution. Leadership, in such circumstances, stays with the bourgeoisie. But this is a vacillating and
conciliatory leadership, especially when bourgeois interests are
hit hard by imperialism and the *latifúndio* and the bourgeoisie
fears the proletariat in its struggle against these two
enemies.

In any case – and above all when confronted with the bourgeois–proletariat alliance – we who follow Marxism-Leninism
have no alternative but to build proletarian strength in order
not to remain subordinated to the bourgeoisie. This strength is
only achieved by working ceaselessly with the proletariat, at its
base, i.e. within industry. If we do not work within industry,
above all within imperialist and state industries, we cannot
strengthen the proletariat. But this is not the only factor in the
growth of our strength. Whatever the circumstances, it is crucial to work on the peasantry, and bring the rural masses into
the struggle as the main ally of the proletariat. The piecemeal
and backward condition of revolutionary work in the countryside is the weakness of the Brazilian revolution and the Marxist
leadership, and the cause of constant failures.

The Brazilian crisis has reached a point where the proletariat cannot expect to solve it alone by peaceful means and
support for the bourgeoisie in the struggle for reform. Such a
method, moreover, could only succeed in Brazil if the Marxist
leadership were equipped with enough firm ideological
grounding to direct the struggle without losing a sense of its
class basis and deflecting the course of the revolution. The
opposite happened however, and the peaceful road through
reforms was blocked by the April the First coup. Now that road
to revolution is done with. To continue along it means adopting

a strategy which will work for the institutionalization of the coup and dictatorship. Such an institutionalization – which is the dictatorship's goal – is designed to paralyse the popular liberation movement, subjugate the proletariat and popular and nationalist forces, and make Brazil a permanent and stable satellite of the US. The two theses of westernization and inter-dependence of sovereignty, invented in response to an eventual Third World War, are the ideological disguise of this institutionalization.

This is the new political move designed by the ruling classes with US collaboration after the April the First coup in order to check the rise of the masses and the liberation of our country from North American influence.

Once again: the adoption of peaceful techniques by the Marxists would prevent them from taking the initiative or any decisive action against the dictatorship and its projects for institutionalizing itself. The dictatorship is founded on force; this has been its sole instrument against the people and the opposition. The only result of a new resort to peaceful means as a solution to the Brazilian crisis would be to force the Marxists into a false position and into eventual collaboration with the dictatorship, to the benefit of the reactionary classes. Besides being superseded by and irrelevant to the forces of nationalism and the people, a peaceful strategy could create another menace, a menace not necessarily ruling out violent repression and military force by the dictatorship. This is the possible identification of the forces of nationalism and the proletariat. In this case, by following a peaceful course, the Marxists would help to turn Brazil into a social democracy acting in the name of the US as a check on the liberation movements of Latin America. Peaceful techniques would at present have the effect of deluding the people and demoralizing popular and nationalist elements who need revolutionary stimulus.

It is obvious that in the face of the tremendous shock of the April coup, the proletariat has no choice but to adopt a revolutionary strategy aimed at the overthrow of the dictatorship. This means revolution: preparation for armed insurrection.

This means non-peaceful means, violence – even civil war. If the masses do not resort to violence the dictatorship will become an institution for an indefinite period.

Without a revolutionary strategy and revolutionary action firmly grounded on politicization at the base and not simply at vanguard level, we cannot create a united front or mobilize the masses under the leadership they need to defeat the dictatorship. A revolutionary strategy – indispensable if we are to escape from apathy and inactivity – needs ceaseless work among the basic forces of the revolution, the proletariat, peasantry, students and intellectuals. Work among the bourgeoisie cannot, within such a strategy, continue to be of primary importance, although it is by no means a question of abandoning it entirely.

A revolutionary strategy must lead to a break with the policy of the subordination of proletariat to bourgeoisie, and to the separation of the proletariat and the bourgeois parties. By acting as an independent force, the Communists and Brazilian Left in general will find their rightful place and triumph taking the masses with them. The so-called Brazilian élites have already been exposed as failures. It would be disastrous for us to try any kind of solution which would compromise our liberty with these 'élites'.

When it comes to working with the revolution's primary forces, the most important work, which must be given priority, is work with the peasantry, shifting the struggle towards the country's interior, creating revolutionary consciousness amongst the peasants. Within the strategic scheme offered by Brazilian reality, the foundations of proletarian action are the peasantry. The peasant–proletariat alliance is the touchstone of the Brazilian revolution. It will mean a great step forward, a substitution of a Marxist strategy for the old bourgeois–proletarian alliance. Within this new strategy, the rural masses will fulfil a decisive role as a support for the urban struggle. This is why we must open a second front. This is why we must not simply limit our action to the cities where, of course, besides liaison work with other groups, we need to be deeply established with the proletariat in the large companies and industries. This is indispensable. But there will be no hope of strategic success without a second front in the country-side.

Another fundamental element in the Marxist strategy is the armed forces and the part they play in the revolution. The possibility of a split in the military – a real possibility in the complex context of Brazilian politics – is important on the strategic level as a probable immediate cause of civil war. Popular and nationalist elements must therefore be absolutely independent in order to have the necessary freedom of action and not to become subservient to one or other of the factions if a civil war develops.

The solution of the chronic Brazilian crisis by armed force on the part of the proletariat requires a hard struggle and sacrifices on the part of the vanguard. It is a radical solution depending always on patient, tenacious and sustained effort among the permanent forces of the revolution. It must count on the eventual support of broad areas of society as discontent grows and the dictatorship progresses towards institutionalization.

Brazilian experience demonstrates the need for insisting on a revolutionary solution. Given our current historical situation, to renounce revolutionary strategy is to compromise the future of Brazil and that of all Latin America.

C. Revolutionary Leadership
and Current Tactics

As we have seen, the point at issue is the resolution of the chronic Brazilian crisis. Today this crisis involves a new situation: its content and development have been created by the growth of capitalism in subservience to imperialism, and by the survival of the *latifúndio*. It is the growth of capitalism in these conditions which has determined the whole political process in Brazil. This capitalist growth has not, of course, freed us from the condition of an underdeveloped country. But there has been a total change in the social situation of Brazil; it is now no longer a country which suffers from a lack of capital but suffers instead from capitalism itself.

North American imperialism operates in Brazil through a section of Brazilian capitalism. In other words, despite differences of interest with the US, Brazilian capitalism is being utilized by North American imperialism, which relies fundamentally on pro-colonialist sections of the bourgeoisie. A section of Brazilian capitalism sees no other solution but to become the economic vassal of the US while others, despite their differences with North American imperialism, are incapable of challenging US interests.

The decisive blow can be made against US imperialism only after the overthrow of the present dictatorship, whose principal function is to represent *latifúndio* interests and those of the sector of the bourgeoisie supporting the US and its policy of westernization, and its preparation for world war.

The conflict between bourgeoisie and proletariat has achieved new dimensions; and this means that we cannot struggle against imperialism or *latifúndio* by nourishing bourgeois illusions or renouncing class struggle against the bourgeoisie. The Brazilian proletariat must act independently, even though, as far as Brazil is concerned, an alliance between bourgeoisie and proletariat is indispensable. The proletariat cannot remain under the hegemony of the bourgeoisie, even if the latter continues to direct the political process due to its control of the process of economic expansion in Brazil.

The basic point to remember in the question as to who will gain control of the Brazilian revolution is not that the bourgeoisie has actual control of the political processes. Neither is it in the fact that we must struggle for leadership of the proletariat as long as this leadership is not in our hands. Rather it consists in recognizing that bourgeois leadership of the revolution is not inevitable; that the proletariat *can* control the revolution from the start, and that we must struggle decisively to win that control. This will not modify the anti-imperialist, anti-feudal, nationalist and democratic nature of the revolution. It will strengthen it. If we cease to struggle to gain control of the revolutionary process, we will at best merely help the bourgeoisie of Brazil to transform the country into a Latin American social democracy, in which case Brazil's role will be merely to help the US check liberation movements in other countries. The state produced by a bourgeois-led revolution will be a bourgeois state, and will not solve the fundamental problems of the revolution: the expulsion of the imperialists and liquidation of the *latifúndio*.

Our mistake under the João Goulart government was that we failed to grasp this. We did not maintain the independence of the proletariat or fight for it, and we trusted the bourgeois leadership. This brought us to defeat and caused a temporary collapse of the revolution. Present-day Brazil is not the Brazil of 1945, 1955 or 1960. It is another Brazil with the bourgeoisie in control within a changed international situation quite unlike that which confronted us immediately after the Second World War.

Our self-criticism cannot start from false premises which

ignore Brazilian historical realities. It cannot start from a non-proletarian class perspective. Correct ideological perspective is a fundamental condition for successful political action. We are at present suffering from a loss of class-consciousness, from a loss of direction within the Brazilian revolution. It is not simply a question of recognizing that we were defeated by the April military coup, that we were weak, that we had no mass movement, that there is no longer any struggle against the coup and that the dictators are crushing us. All this is true, but our main obligation is to present a concrete analysis and solution in accordance with Marxist strategies and tactics.

We must initiate revolutionary strategies. And for this we must overthrow the current dictatorship, which cannot be done if we wait for it to institutionalize itself through elections. There is now no alternative in Brazil; daily experience is making plain that the dictatorship can only be overthrown by force. North American imperialism will not stand by while the dictatorship or any other pro-imperialist government is overthrown, just as it did not stand by in Dominica. It will take to violence and armed intervention whenever it feels its position threatened. North American imperialism will not abandon without a struggle the position it won in Brazil by means of the military coup. A revolutionary strategy in Brazil must abide by a major principle: it must reject all thoughts of a peaceful solution and realize that force is the only possible way of overthrowing the dictatorship.

But a revolutionary strategy is not in itself enough to lead the popular and nationalist forces into battle. We also need a tactical programme drawn up in the light of our strategy and dependent upon it. We cannot draw up ambiguous tactical plans valid for a peaceful or violent solution alike. Ambiguous tactics lead to a rapid loss of prestige and authority on our part, and bewilderment in the face of events.

No one imagines we can call the masses now to popular insurrection. Nothing would happen. Neither would there be any advantage in confronting the dictatorship, launching the struggle and suffering their violence and counter-attacks if we continue to maintain that we are aiming at a peaceful solution. That would be like promising heaven to people on earth.

Any short-term tactic issuing from a revolutionary strategy is itself revolutionary; which means it has no truck with sectarianism and conventional leftism. Such a tactic will aim at bringing the masses out to fight against the dictatorship and replace it with an effective democratic government. The means to be used are such means as the masses will accept. But the Communists must give an example of revolutionary impetus – which they clearly will not do by going into the fight with a strategy aiming at a peaceful solution. A revolutionary tactic embraces all aspects of political struggle and is simultaneously capable of controlling all the basic forces of the revolution. It is a popular tactic, a mass-tactic, clearly intelligible to all – not a tactic for the privileged or experts in revolutionary matters, nor a tactic based on juggling dogmatic formulae. It is not a tactic which turns up complicated explanations for every new political circumstance, or issues directives which lead nowhere, raise no revolutionary enthusiasm and lead to no real confrontation. This is what we have been having for the last two years under the dictatorship. It is not a tactic which leads to political and electoral compromises and feeds bourgeois illusions, invites conformism and apathy. Revolutionary tactics are tactics for mass struggle and their purpose is to advance the basic strategic objectives they serve. They are tactics designed to bring about the overthrow of the dictatorship as its first objective and to realize the strategic aims of the nationalist and popular forces.

These tactics do not, for the present, prevent us from remaining within the Brazilian political process, even though they are revolutionary. They do not rule out a relentless struggle for a united and anti-dictatorship front or making use of what limited legal means are available. They do not prevent our utilizing any opening which may offer itself in the political process and lead to our exposing the dictatorship and the electoral farce. They do not rule out our participation in conflicts within the ruling classes or the military where there may be fissures and dissension, violent disagreements and even civil war. We must not allow ourselves to get out of touch with the political situation of the moment and fail to create conditions necessary to put political initiative into our or the masses' hands.

Our tactics require constant work in industry and especially among the peasants – a condition for the peasant–proletariat alliance – and work amongst the armed forces and in tellectuals. These are the permanent features of a Marxist tactic which will work for the creation of organized proletarian strength. Without such strength we cannot influence the political process or win any kind of important victory within the revolution. The creation of proletarian strength requires struggle in the towns and in the countryside. The key to the struggle against the dictatorship and to transforming the mass movements lies in the peasant struggle. Hence the importance of work in the countryside in the context of the tactic; an importance deriving from the fact that through it will come the possibility of linking the political struggle in the cities with rural political struggle in Brazil for the first time.

We will not move decisively against the dictatorship unless we overcome the contempt commonly held for work among the peasants, and grasp the importance of the peasants in the revolutionary struggle. The struggle cannot be fought with the weapons of democracy and nationalism alone, nor by divorcing one or both of these from the struggle for the land and for peasant interests. It is an error to put off the struggle for peasant interests until the revolution is in its decisive stage. Work in the countryside is tactical work. It is the essential factor, an indispensable part of proletarian tactics.

D. Some Tactical Principles
for the Present Situation

Besides the permanent tactical principles of Marxism, which aim at creating armed proletarian strength, there are some general principles relevant to the current situation in Brazil which refer to practical methods of mobilizing the revolution's permanent forces and the united front.

Among them the principle of retreat is of great importance. At no point should a tactical move be made without the certain availability of a sure line of retreat. As far as the idea of offensive is concerned, experience shows that it is not always necessary to advance whenever one has achieved some victory or partial success. There are inevitably times when we should call a halt and consolidate our strength in order to advance again.

When the political offensive is in enemy hands the revolutionary forces must try to open another front under proletarian control. This second front, aimed at taking the initiative out of the enemy's hands, can be in any area, but will only speed a qualitative change in the political struggle if it is an active front opened in rural areas among the peasants.

Another important principle concerns the problem of proletarian strength. Whenever it takes any political initiative the proletariat must at the same time concentrate on building up its own strength. Proletarian strength depends on ideological and political work in industry, among the peasants, military, intellectuals, students and women, and among the youth and middle strata in the large cities.

One of the right ways to tactical success is for the proletariat never to fail to create its own forces and strengthen itself at rank-and-file level as soon as it begins acting in the united front. Otherwise the proletariat cannot be sure of its own independence. Without its own forces the proletariat will be a plaything in bourgeois hands.

If proletarian forces are to be used correctly there must be a combined effort in industry, and among peasants and the military forces. If not, proletarian tactics will go astray. The proletariat cannot be victorious alone without the backing of a united anti-dictatorship front and without the latter being supported by a proletarian–peasant alliance.

A general political strike by the proletariat on a national basis, unsupported by peasantry and military, popular masses, students, intellectuals etc., will produce no results since it means throwing the proletariat into the struggle alone. On the other hand, victory is impossible if the revolutionary movement depends solely on peasant struggle isolated from urban struggle, or solely on military struggle or action by the military in alliance with proletarian forces. As far as the military is concerned, there is no question of succeeding among them if political work in military circles is influenced by bourgeois ideology or revolutionary nationalism and not by proletarian ideology.

As far as the united front is concerned, it must be remembered that it cannot be seen simply as a group of parties or ex-parties opposed to the dictatorship. The class composition of the united front must be kept in view, as well as the political tendencies and forces the parties and – not the least – their leaders represent. In this connection it is important to recognize the existence of three forces inside the united front: the centre or middle-of-the-road forces which comprise most of the bourgeoisie and its allies; the Left and radical group; and opposite them the rightist elements in the united front. If we lose sight of this distinction action in the front becomes difficult. Above all it is impossible to carry out positive work in the united front if we limit our efforts to political activity at leadership level or to compromises with the centre forces. Poltical activity at the top does not bring victories. The main need is for work at ground level among the proletariat, which needs tenacity and determination on the part of proletarian leaders.

Another consideration is the principle of unity and struggle with the bourgeoisie within the united front. This can be applied only if the proletariat unleashes the class struggle and successfully manages the struggle of the democratic and nationalist masses which includes the struggle for the land. The proletariat must adopt a clearly defined revolutionary posture and in no circumstances is there room for it as a moderating influence inside the national front. If it takes this position the proletariat straggles behind the bourgeoisie.

Our task is not to destroy the centre forces or to make them, rather than the imperialists, our main target. The danger lies in allying ourselves with them alone and neglecting the radical forces; such a course would leave us at the centre's mercy.

It is a mistake to underestimate the value of an alliance with the radical groups. Brazilian radicalism is the fruit of the advance of the revolutionary movement and of extreme resistance to the dictators. By proposing a revolutionary strategy and a tactical plan within the strategy we shall attract the radical forces in the united front towards the proletariat. The aim is unity within the Left. An important factor in this unity of the Left, as opposed to unity with the Centre, is an alliance with the Catholics and the Catholic Left in particular. Similarly, unity with the revolutionary nationalists is also indispensable, with the followers of Brizola, Arrais, Julião and others, as with other leftist currents opposed to the dictators. In this respect the North-East is worth special attention. Thanks to their well-known resistance to cultural terrorism, the intellectuals are tending towards the Left and unity with them is indispensable. In fact successful unity with the centre anti-dictatorship forces including those led by Goulart, Quadros, Kubitschek etc., *depends* on unity with the Left. The proletariat cannot reject alliance with the centre forces of the united front. But if it rejects alliance with the Left it will have no strength to attract the centre and unite with it.

Another important tactical principle regarding the united front is that of unity of programme and action; and here the starting-point is the need for a consistent line in united front declarations about the overthrow of the dictators. The prerequisite for this is the united anti-dictatorship front itself, which must be as broad as possible and count on *all* the political and class forces opposed to the dictatorship. Even if these forces happen to act independently, their actions must converge on the main objective.

The principle of unity of programme and action does not, however, mean the destruction of any group within the front, nor does it rule out the right of mutual constructive criticism.

Whatever the circumstances, the proletariat together with the Communists must initiate and support the struggle against the dictatorship and so bring the nationalist and popular forces into the battle. We must commit the forces of the anti-imperialist, anti-feudal, democratic and national revolution to struggle against the dictatorship. Within these basic forces we must give priority to the peasants, who must not be thrown into the fight only when revolutionary state power has actually been won – i.e., when the goals of the long-term strategy are being achieved. It must be done straight away: this is the importance of the peasant struggle and their claims and role in the national and democratic struggle. Herein lies the importance of the struggle for the land and the peasant's part in the political struggle against the dictators. This approach does not, as some imagine, imply a change in the nature of the revolution; nor does it imply the predominance of the agrarian problem over the nationalist and anti-imperialist aspect of the struggle.

The strategic perspective of the current historical phase remains unchanged since the basic problems up to now have remained unsolved. The fundamental condition for developing the struggle is to deploy every kind of offensive and organization at once, both legal and illegal, and to use any legal possibilities to further nationalist and democratic demands, including peasant demands. This means firm action wherever there are popular groups – in the unions, women's groups, student and peasant organizations etc. The purpose of such action will be to initiate and support confrontation and stimulate mass combativity. The mainstay of combined struggle and organization is a clear recognition of the importance of the peasant struggle and the need for a second front in Brazilian politics.

It is a fundamental in Marxist tactics to ensure that at any stage of the proletarian struggle the aim must be to achieve a government which will open the way to total national liberation – economic, political and social – for the people, and to a final solution of the basic strategic problem.

In the Brazilian situation we must fight for a government which will replace the present dictatorship. And this must be a genuinely democratic government. It must be the opposite of what we have now. All other tasks must be subordinated to this.

The Communists' tactics, based on the proletariat, are today totally different from their previous tactics. Before, they were conditioned by the country's peaceful evolution. Today's are shaped by the knowledge that the dictatorship can only be overthrown by force and that we will eventually have to face violence and armed aggression from US imperialism. The situation we are facing is completely new. Our tactics also must be new.

E. Against Tactics which Subordinate Proletariat to Bourgeoisie

The proletariat cannot indiscriminately follow any tactical line. It must reject all those which do not work towards the main objectives of the anti-imperialist, anti-feudal, democratic and nationalist revolution. Any tactical line followed in the country's present situation which leads to the ideological subordination of proletariat to bourgeoisie must be condemned. Everyone knows that these incorrect ideological lines exist, and have arisen from bourgeois influences on the proletariat. We need to become acquainted with their main theses in order to combat their inroads into revolutionary circles.

The main tactical line of this kind merely envisages the alliance of proletariat and bourgeoisie and fails to move beyond this narrow ideal. It is an intrinsically half-hearted and non-progressive tactical line due to its distrust and lack of confidence in the proletariat. Its premise is an acceptance of the idea that Brazilian politics are *de facto* controlled by the bourgeoisie and will remain so. It is the line which looks for moderate solutions and fears radical struggle and revolutionary solutions, in case the latter alienate the bourgeoisie and damage long-term collaboration with them.

The tactic we are discussing sticks religiously to old-fashioned theoretical canons and sees no hope of starting the revolution save when or if the pre-revolutionary conditions of classical revolutionary theory come into existence. The Cuban revolution destroyed this traditional notion, but the tactic we are talking about ignores such new facts.

As far as self-criticism goes, the tactic in question does not start from a class perspective. It rejects the idea that the main mistake of the Communists in the past was the deluded faith they placed in bourgeois leadership. It is reluctant to admit we are still basically under bourgeois leadership and its half-hearted pressures for compromise. It will not face up to the fact that we are losing our influence on the masses, and giving them the lie that it was we who were previously in power and that we were the same thing as Goulart. Due to our ideological subservience to the bourgeoisie we fell into the political trap of supporting Goulart's positive actions and attacking his negative ones. This is wrong; and its wrongness lies in waiting on bourgeois initiatives and doing nothing to get out of a policy of conformism. There is no question of rejecting a united front with the bourgeoisie. But an intrinsic condition of such a front as far as we are concerned is that it must fight for proletarian supremacy within it so as not to be dragged along behind the bourgeoisie.

The tactic we are rejecting here is not worried by these problems. Its main concern – derived from the idea that we are a moderating force – lies in another direction: to remain alert against left-wing deviation. This deviation was, in fact, a spontaneous reaction to the impossibility of achieving an advanced programme by trusting the bourgeoisie rather than working with the basic forces of the revolution. While maintaining that leftism was the main cause of our mistakes, the tactic in question continues to make a few attacks on rightist deviation at least for form's sake. All that this policy achieves is the division of the proletariat into two right and left factions. It remains an unconvincing policy, and its worst result is a refusal to examine the main cause of our mistakes which has been a loss of class consciousness.

By failing to see that our worst misfortunes come from trying to keep going with our umbilical cord still tied to the bourgeoisie, the tactic in question will not dare to accept violent overthrow of the dictatorship as a basic policy. But this is the only correct policy: Brazilian experience shows that dictators can only be overthrown by force. Even in other circumstances violence will still be necessary because North American imperialism will use force if its interests are threatened.

The tactic under criticism, however, envisages the undermining and isolating of the dictatorship until it is too weak to use violence against the people and can be overthrown without armed struggle being the principal mode of action. It accepts this because it still puts its faith in the bourgeoisie and expects that internal conflict within the ruling classes will produce a favourable conclusion for the people without need for radical struggle. This is why the said tactic keeps on talking of 'mass struggle' as the way to overthrow the dictatorship – in order to avoid the idea of a violent overthrow of the dictators. Everyone talks about mass struggle against the dictators. It is the most elementary and uncontroversial idea currently in circulation. What people would like to know is what this 'mass struggle' will be.

The tactic under discussion defines mass struggle for the overthrow of the dictatorship as participation in elections, protests, strikes, demonstrations, etc. As a climax to this it envisages a general political strike without recourse to armed struggle, popular insurrection or civil war. In other words it supposes that in current conditions a political campaign could triumph through elections, strikes and protests in all of which decisive mass action could be carried out peacefully. This is the triumph of class illusion, a truly Panglossian delusion which can only be explained by the fact that the said tactic believes that one of the factions within the ruling classes will eventually seek the proletariat's help to free itself from the threat of other factions in the battle for political power. Thus the overthrow of the dictatorship would be the result of bourgeois struggle and bourgeois leadership – or that of a section of the bourgeoisie – which would eventually call on proletarian support and avoid bloodshed or violence.

Incredible as it may seem, this same tactic also envisages armed struggle. In fact it even insists on it frequently. But with one reservation about the proper moment for unleashing armed struggle which, its proponents constantly argue, must not be used now but only when the right moment arises – when it should become the main form of struggle. This approach demonstrates that the tactic in question will use every possible means to bring about the peaceful overthrow of the dictatorship even at the cost of ideological subjection of proletariat to bourgeoisie. Only when these means are exhausted, the argument goes, will the moment for armed struggle have arrived.

By adopting this attitude the tactic under review confuses the forms that the struggle will take with the tactical path to be followed. The point does not lie in defining in advance the forms the struggle will take, or in enumerating them or selecting some and rejecting others, nor in accepting them all at once.

The key is the tactical line – in knowing which combination of techniques will lead to the overthrow of the dictatorship through mass action and with a strengthening of the independent position of the proletariat. The link can only be work in the rural sector, a thorough penetration of Brazilian rural areas and a preparation for peasant struggle with all the consequences arising from activities against imperialism and *latifúndio*. The tactic we are criticizing ignores the peasants' place in the battle against the dictatorship precisely because it fears a radicalization of the political process. And this is because when it comes to its combat programme it only puts forward demands connected with nationalism, democratic freedoms and proletarian interests. Peasant demands are omitted. The struggle for the land is to be put off until the decisive stages of the struggle for revolutionary state power. This approach shows that the said tactic believes only in urban struggle – which means that it persists in the idea that the proletariat can be thrown into the battle without peasant support, which is what has happened up to now in the Brazilian revolutionary movement. The tactical line under discussion fails to see that the peasantry are the cornerstone in Brazil as in all Latin America.

As far as the electoral process is concerned, the line in

question goes wrong because it does not trust in the proletariat and bows down to the bourgeoisie and its leaders. Everyone can see that the way to overthrowing the dictatorship does not lie in elections. This has been proved by experience, since the dictatorship has used force, e.g. special decrees and the like, to turn the elections into a farce.

Nevertheless, the tactic under review would like to use the elections to inflict local defeats on the dictatorship to weaken it and hasten its collapse. To achieve this it would support such anti-dictatorship groups as deserve the confidence of the people. If this became impossible it would try blank votes and similar exposures of the electoral farce. Which points to a curious fact: the tactic in question does not think the methods already used by the dictators to block a possible electoral victory by popular candidates are in themselves sufficient. Because it is obvious that candidates who have been accepted by the dictatorship or have compromised with it cannot be called popular. . . . And they are the only ones likely to be unaffected by the disqualifying laws and other fascist electoral devices.

To expect that elections called by the dictatorship will lead to its partial defeat and to an undermining of the régime and the eventual recapture of the democratic process without bloodshed and sustained struggle, would lead the Brazilian proletariat up the blind alley of electoral delusions, leaving them to drift miserably under command of the régime's elected representatives or of supporters of the April military coup. And this is the line defended by people who have themselves experienced the people's rejection of the government and its policies.

This is all the tactical line we are discussing has to offer as a solution to the problem of the overthrow of the dictatorship. It will lead the revolutionary movement into utter delusion and bewilderment, or cause it to stagnate in the sluggish waters of bourgeois politics.

So far as possible government crises are concerned, supporters of this line admit as a premise that further coups are possible. This is a real possibility. But if another coup is at-

tempted this tactical line wants the popular forces to intervene
to avoid a *reactionary solution* which would strengthen Cas-
telo and replace the old instigators of the coup. In other words,
the tactical line we are criticizing does not consider that Cas-
telo is sufficiently reactionary or powerful at the present —
although he might *become so* through a new coup. The other
way by which a reactionary situation might develop, the tactic
argues, is through the emergence of new forces as a result of a
coup. The ideological basis of this tactic is dominated by un-
grounded optimism about the current situation and by hopes
for a *volte face* by the bourgeoisie, who would then work for a
democratic solution.

In conclusion, the discussion of this tactic demonstrates that
the proletariat has no part in it and, if the proletariat were
foolish enough to adopt it as a programme, it would remain
bewildered and drift aimlessly without a clear response to the
policies, whims and violence of the dictatorship. That is why
the struggle against ideological subordination of proletariat to
bourgeoisie and the rejection of a policy based on this principle
is an essential part of the fight to bring down the dictatorship.

F. The Proletariat and the Military Forces

The proletariat can never neglect the military forces, and must adopt a position towards and a policy for them.

In this connection Engels, in his work *The Role of Violence in History*, states the following: 'In politics there are only two decisive forces: organized state force, i.e. the army; and disorganized force, i.e. the fundamental strength of the popular masses.' Thus in Marxist terms the military forces are the organized strength of the state. For the proletariat to define its position towards the military it must see them as an intrinsic element of the state apparatus, as an instrument of state power designed and organized with the objective of ensuring the supremacy of the classes that state represents. Thus the nature of the state determines the nature of its armed forces. The state will never organize or allow to be organized military forces opposed to it or likely to hinder its class supremacy. Military forces have a repressive and conservative class function.

Throughout its history the Brazilian state has organized and used its military forces with the express design of guaranteeing the domination of ruling classes in the country. Within this design, however, the Brazilian military is significant in that it also reflects the class struggle of the society we live in. This is due to the military's own composition; it inevitably includes members of the various social classes of Brazilian society. The main component of the military is enlisted from the proletariat and peasantry. The commanding élite comes from the petty bourgeoisie, bourgeoisie and *latifúndio*. Capitalist expansion in Brazil played its part in modifying the composite position and evolution of the armed forces. In certain circumstances (e.g. under the Goulart government) non-aristocratic elements rose into sectors of the military command hitherto closed to commoners, but despite this the military forces have maintained their traditional class structure in Brazil.

Although the military forces are not a coherent whole they do not simply reflect the contradictions of Brazilian society. The state has given them an ideological and political leadership – a class leadership – which prevents them from changing their political course in response to events in society. To this end it established a system of hierarchy and discipline aimed at freeing the armed forces from the various conflicts within society. Nevertheless, the state has not always been successful in this. History records moments when the military forces were brought round to a change of attitude as a result of the failure of the ruling classes to defend their previous positions. The abolition of slavery and the proclamation of the Republic were two such events which demonstrated the possibility of a change of position by the military. Clearly, since they respond to class conflicts within society, the armed forces have also influenced and pressured the ruling classes and came, in fact, to exercise a governing role. It was a progressive role, since the causes they defended signified a real step forward for the country.

Similarly, in recent post-war years the military played a positive role when they supported by an immense majority the state monopolies and other nationalist and even democratic policies, e.g. the November the Eleventh Constitution. The military forces can be progressive only when their activities are not likely to limit or threaten the supremacy of the ruling classes. The same can occur when the power of the old ruling classes disappears or is taken from them – provided that there is no danger of a transfer of state control and machinery to popular hands.

The abolition of slavery, for example, and the proclamation of the Republic weakened the old slave-owning classes. But they still kept the Brazilian state under the control of the ex-

ploiting classes in the name of a reconciliation between bourgeoisie and landowners, which has characterized our
historical evolution ever since. So it was that in the case of the
conflict over oil and other democratic lines backed by a majority in the armed forces after their support of the November
the Eleventh Constitution, the Brazilian state was never actually under any kind of threat and its structures remained unchanged.

Confronted with the advance of the masses threatening to
influence the power structure, or faced with a possible change
of state structure, the ruling classes will bring out the military
against the masses. They will do this, in the last resort, by
unleashing a military coup, destroying democratic freedoms
and annihilating those elements within the army which actually or allegedly favour the people, nationalism and democracy.
This is what happened in the coup of April 1964, prepared
within the armed forces with encouragement and inspiration
from North American imperialism.

Military coups in Brazil cannot be separated from imperialist activities. This became more obvious after the Second
World War when the US redoubled its effort inside the military. In this connection one may recall the speech made by
Adalgiza Néry before the Legislative Assembly of Guanabara
State, published in *Bulletin of the Legislative Assembly of
Guanabara,* 13 November 1964, from which one can infer the
disastrous consequences brought upon us by the signing and
ratification of the US–Brazil Military Treaty.

Nelson Werneck Sodré also makes a significant comment on
p. 403 of his study *Military History of Brazil*:

This is doubtless imperialism's great task: to transform the armed
forces of each nation into an occupation force on its own behalf. To
this end they manipulate anti-communism through constant top-
level meetings between military chiefs, special personnel courses,
study-tours and, above all, military missions. To destroy communism by armed force is to be the fundamental mission of the armed
forces of the 'Western Christian world', and for this the forces will
be given a unique status under a unified command, stripped of all

national characteristics and made indifferent to the specific problems of the countries they represent. Although this continuous and
methodical brainwashing cannot affect every individual in the
armed forces, it has in fact affected certain specialized and therefore
vulnerable groups like the Higher Command and General Staff and
some special services. What has been happening in our case is a
carefully planned and executed campaign to win over the military
command since, when this has been captured, in institutions like the
army with a vertical structure working downwards through hierarchies and discipline, the rest will follow. It must be admitted in
fact that imperialism has been having spectacular successes in this
direction.

The influence and supremacy of North American imperialism
inside the leadership of the Brazilian military is exercising an
extremely negative influence on the country. Facts show that
through this supremacy the military's repressive tendencies
have risen to too high a level in the current situation. It is
beyond question that, as a result of their petty-bourgeois
background and the shock of contact with Brazilian realities,
some officers of the military élite have gone over to Marxism.
But it would be absurd to ignore the constant and growing
numbers of officers employed in torturing, beating and other
Nazi practices within all three forces.

The important point is that reactionary and fascist tendencies in the armed forces had been growing and eventually
came to predominate among the leadership and officers in the
military who were responsible for the April coup. These tendencies ultimately produced the notorious theses of 'geo-
political unity' and 'interdependence of national sovereignty',
both a cover for US imperialism and an insult to Brazilian
national feeling.

Despite the fact that a section of the military does not
accept these tendencies, we must recognize that the bulk of the
armed forces is adapting itself to them, due to fears aroused by
the anti-Communist campaign.

A common mistake among Communists and the Left in general has been the idea that the Brazilian military is democratic

or has a democratic tradition. In Marxist terms this thesis, in view both of the present and of the historical role of the military, has no substance. Once again, in fact, it is an illusion fostered by precisely those groups who should have resisted it most intensely. It has no Marxist value because Marxism approaches reality from a historical and class perspective and a class analysis shows that the Brazilian armed forces have constantly sided with the ruling classes and have up to now been their main protection and salvation in difficult times. We must insist on the thesis that the military forces are identified with the state and have a rigidly defined class status and a repressive function against the rising mass movement. It is this repressive function which creates anti-popular coups within it.

Another controversial question is whether it is possible to win the total support of the military in the battle for the Brazilian revolution. The Marxist reply to this is no, since otherwise we would have to abandon the thesis that the armed forces viewed collectively are an instrument of state repression and are identified with the state. There is no example in history of a revolution – popular or nationalist–democratic and proletarian-led – winning with the outright aid of all the armed forces of a completely reactionary or even bourgeois–democratic state.

Once we have discounted the hopeless mirage of winning over the whole of the armed forces to the revolution, the task remains for the proletariat of adopting a military policy aimed at attracting sections of the conventional armed forces to its cause. This is an objective which can be achieved. We must remember that the armed forces are built up of members of social classes and reflect the conflicts and tensions of Brazilian society, and are therefore themselves liable to internal tension and divisions. And although a majority of the armed forces will continue to stand with the reactionaries, there will always be a section, however small, which can be won over.

As in the case of political leadership it is crucial that the proletariat should avoid putting itself into a position of subservience to the bourgeoisie in formulating its military policy. Bourgeois leadership, even when one of the bourgeois groups in or out of power attempts to carry through a programme of reforms, is vacillating leadership which fears the masses and the proletariat. It is a leadership which experiments with struggle but ends up by capitulating as soon as the forces of the coup raise their head – as happened under João Goulart's government. In the field of military policies the proletariat will suffer inevitable defeat whenever it subordinates its activities to bourgeois leadership or cherishes illusions about an alliance between military and proletariat (*sindicatos*).

This was one of the greatest mistakes made by the popular nationalist forces during the Goulart government, when our military policy was being directed by the bourgeois sections of the executive. Members of the military who supported this line, and ended up by being thrown out of the armed forces by the present dictatorship, have this criticism to make of themselves in an important document: 'we even fell into non-progressive positions and lost ideological direction by thinking we could maintain control of the military within bourgeois leadership'. 'Within bourgeois leadership' here obviously means 'under bourgeois leadership'. It is useless to expect anything from the armed forces under bourgeois leadership, since the bourgeoisie will always pull back because of its fear of giving an opening to the proletariat.

In this document the military men referred to conclude that the policy of military subordination to bourgeois command led to confusion in the face of events on 31 March 1964, when the April coup was launched, and ultimately resulted in their failure to resist even with the means still available to them.

Those who adopt a compromise military policy are refusing a class perspective and rejecting the essential tenets of Marxism–Leninism. They are also rejecting the spirit of proletarian class solidarity when they preach a conventionally leftish military policy. These are the people who claim that the purpose of military policy is to lead the armed struggle, destroy the state *and* the armed forces themselves.

In the present conditions anyone who defends this kind of policy inside the armed forces ends up in isolation.

Correct military policy consists of a permanent tactical

application of revolutionary strategy. This means uniting revolutionary elements in the armed forces with the proletariat,
peasantry and basic forces of the revolution. Military struggle
must be combined with working-class and peasant struggle in
line with the tactics and strategy of the proletariat. By military
struggle we are also referring here to conflict within the armed
forces. When we speak of revolutionary elements within the
army we do so precisely because the military can never be
wholly revolutionary, but only a section can ever be won over.
On the other hand when we speak of *military* struggle we do
not mean the same as armed struggle in general, since the
latter includes civilian elements and can even develop into
peasant struggle. All this means that armed struggle need not
necessarily be conducted under military leadership.

A military policy which merely considers the armed forces in
isolation, and tries to develop within them political work divorced from extra-military revolutionary work, has little chance
of success. In view of this and the proviso that military policy
must never be subordinated to bourgeois command, it remains
to outline a tactic to be used within the armed forces. In this
connection the above-quoted document states: 'we conceive of
tactics within the armed forces as being of two types: one a
broad-based, legal mass tactic; the other a clandestine tactic'.
As far as the former is concerned we must not hinder patriots
struggling inside the armed forces (and outside them also) for a
change in the function of the Brazilian military. And the proletariat must press for these changes without yielding to pressures and misgivings emanating from the bourgeoisie, who fear
the adoption of a nationalist and democratic political line by
the military.

On p. 104 of Sodré's *Military History of Brazil*, there
appears an outline of such a programme to which we refer
readers. Its basic point is the creation of professional demands
in a democratic direction, i.e. demands for a democratization
of the military structures and for the transfer of military supplies to national control. This point is made clear by Sodré on
p. 407 of his work:

It is becoming abundantly clear to everyone that the armed forces' matériel can never be adequately supplied from outside by interests not identified with our own. We need to produce equipment in line with our own needs, and supplies for the armed forces must keep in line with the material development of our country and should not be fetched from abroad, so worsening our trade debt to a degree which is now coming to be felt as intolerable. Consequently, we must not only put equipment and matériel under national control, but also its production and the knowledge required for its use.

From the masses' point of view such claims are the foundation of a correct military policy. As far as the clandestine tactics within the armed forces are concerned, the following relevant passage from the document mentioned above may be quoted: 'The basic illegal tactic must centre on the creation of an alternative coordinating leadership independent of bourgeois control.' The idea of a dual tactic inside the armed forces does not mean that each should act independently. On the contrary, they should both collaborate to achieve the same objective: the isolation of the military Right.

G. Guerrilla Warfare and Its Use

The basic technique of the Brazilian people against the dictators is mass resistance. There is no need here to elaborate on the techniques of mass resistance, since they were discussed in the book *Why I Fought against Imprisonment* in the chapter on 'The Role of the Nationalist and Popular Forces'.

Guerrilla warfare in Brazil is one of the techniques of mass resistance. It is a type of complementary struggle which will not in itself bring final victory. Both in ordinary warfare and in revolutionary struggle, guerrilla warfare is a supplementary form of combat. History shows that guerrilla conflict, in this role, has played an important part in liberating peoples and overthrowing tyranny. It is, of course, familiar to us in Brazil from its use against the Dutch invasion. The guerrilla campaigns led by Luiz Barbalho were designed to destroy the foreign enemy's supply sources. Barbalho marched from Rio Grande do Norte to Bahia, passing through the enemy's lines to reach Fort Barbalho in the city of Salvador. His guerrilla campaign was combined with a burnt-earth policy which hindered the enemy's food supply. But what finally decided the issue and brought about the expulsion of the Dutch were the great battles of Monte das Tabocas and Montes Guararapes, and the final encirclement of the invaders which culminated in the surrender at Campina de Taborda. Other examples may be quoted such as the campaign against the Napoleonic invasion in Spain, China's war against the Japanese and the civil war against Chiang Kai-Shek, Cuba and the campaign led by Fidel Castro and Che Guevara.

Where there is no regular army yet in existence, a persistent and prolonged guerrilla campaign leads to the formation of a regular army, providing the campaign is well managed and conditions are right. Guerrilla struggle thus constitutes a tactic in line with revolutionary strategy, aimed at bringing the nationalist and popular forces to victory.

It is also one form of political struggle. But it is a form of struggle applicable only when the political struggle can no longer be conducted by peaceful means. Although insurrection and civil war are also ways of furthering the political struggle, guerrilla warfare doubtless has the advantage of being rapidly organized and of needing to begin with relatively small forces. The guerrilla campaign can also speedily be coordinated with the other two techniques of insurrection and civil war.

Nationalist and popular forces need power. This is why the time is right to use guerrilla warfare in combination with the other techniques still available in the cities. By available techniques we mean all kinds of protest and demonstrations, even though the dictatorship will repress them by violence. Implicit in all this, of course, is a recognition of the fact that guerrilla warfare is not the right technique for urban areas,* for it is designed for rural areas where there is room for manoeuvre and the war can spread out. A guerrilla war which cannot expand is not fulfilling its purpose.

The political struggle in Brazil has undergone a change. There is no longer any real hope of winning it by electoral methods or through mass pressure on the government. We need to realize that there is no connection between the use of legal means and the achievement of ultimate victory.

Nevertheless, however limited these possibilities, they should never be despised.

Since April 1964 we have been living under a military dictatorship which uses violence and terror to suppress the people. Severe penalties are imposed by the courts on its opponents, and they are stiffer penalties than the ones dealt out

* It must be remembered that this passage was written in late 1965. (Translator's note.)

under the New State (*Estado Novo*).* Repressive laws such as the dissolution of political parties are rigidly enforced. Emergency decrees appear one after the other. Elections and the candidates' powers have become mere concessions from the dictators, who have also introduced the device of indirect elections and the disqualification of non-approved candidates. All this has meant the destruction of the so-called representative system and the transformation of the elections into a farce. Individual and social rights have been destroyed; the Constitution has been torn up and arbitrary laws substituted in its place. Power is in the hands of fascist colonels who have absolute control over the Military and Police Courts (IPM), and they interfere constantly with civil processes. Thousands of Brazilians, civilian and military, have lost their political rights and are prevented from finding work suited to their talents. The dictators have reduced them to the level of outcasts.

The group in power is busily setting up military courts, interrogating suspects, arresting, sentencing and ignoring *habeas corpus* orders. Elsewhere they are busily introducing fascist laws, following US dictates and applying disastrous financial policies which are paralysing the country, burdening the people with taxes, creating shortages (without curing inflation), while they hand the country over to North American trusts and monopolies and – ultimately – to US control. Given such a picture, it is not difficult to see how the social and economic situation of Brazil is likely to oblige us to take to guerrilla and civil war.

The factors at work in Brazil which led to the defeat of the nationalist and popular forces and which may now involve us in guerrilla war are not unconnected with the international situation which has had special repercussions on Latin America. These new factors arise from the general crisis of capitalism and from the problems facing national liberation movements in a situation of global *détente*. One of the most characteristic factors is the transformation of the armed forces of certain underdeveloped or recently decolonized countries into defence organizations for US imperialism and the reactionary forces

* Of Getulio Vargas, dictator 1930–45.

within each country. After the 1964 coup in Brazil we had military coups in Algeria, Indonesia and the Congo. The process of using a country's armed forces against democracy and popular liberation is going on continually. Now they have put aside illusory hopes for an easy victory and are in a position to analyse why they were surprised by military coups, revolutionaries will strive to rectify their mistakes and apply new forms of struggle. Some oppressed peoples will use guerrilla warfare and switch the struggle to rural areas, so opening a second front.

Present experience with mass struggle demonstrates the importance of a shift in the struggle towards the interior, without losing sight of the urban proletariat, and the need to transform the anti-dictatorship movement. It is in the countryside, among the rural masses, that we will find the right conditions for the struggle which we must now initiate. It is certain that the urban struggle will grow, despite repression and persecution from the dictatorship. But by infiltrating the countryside revolutionaries will be able to bring the peasantry into the battle in support of the urban masses.

One favourable factor is that, in several Latin American countries where the peasantry and members of exploited Indian racial groups are in the majority, guerrilla warfare is tending to concentrate on areas bordering the Brazilian hinterland; and this will certainly have repercussions on our rural masses. The certainty as far as Brazilian revolutionaries are concerned is that the decisive struggle will depend on the initiative of groups working within the country. There is nothing to support the notion of a guerrilla war arising from anywhere but the peasant and mass movement in Brazil. Consequently a factor of decisive importance – one of the most basic in guerrilla tactics – is the closest possible identification with the customs, dress and psychology of the peasantry.

Guerrilla war is an irregular war having nothing in common with conventional warfare, and therefore counts on assistance, shelter and sympathy from the people. Consequently guerrilla warfare is essentially voluntary, and rejects any kind of coercion or conscription as a means of ensuring its expansion.

In the present conditions the mission of guerrilla warfare will be to harass the repressive forces, involve the peasantry in political and class struggle, and bring them into the fight against the dictators. Guerrilla warfare is one of the ways of carrying the struggle for land and freedom into the interior, and of introducing to the peasantry the campaign against North American imperialism and the injustices of the *latifúndio* and the fight for a minimum of comfort and decency for the exploited rural masses. Brazil is a country controlled by a pro-colonialist military dictatorship and by North American imperialism served by traitors who have taken power. Guerrilla warfare in Brazil will inevitably signify a protest against this control and a point of reference for an eventual people's rising. It would be unpardonable to deny it continued support and to refuse to deploy it even where the enemy's forces are superior, or to refuse to allow it to go into battle against the reactionaries.

No one expects guerrilla warfare to be a signal for a popular rising or for a sudden proliferation of insurrectional *focos*. This it certainly will not be. Guerrilla warfare will be a stimulus to the resistance struggle everywhere and will intensify the fight for a united anti-dictatorship front. It will stimulate a final collective effort by the Brazilian people which will lead to the overthrow of the dictatorship.

CHAPTER 2

Letter to the Executive Committee of the Brazilian Communist Party

Dear Comrades,

I am writing to resign from the Executive Committee. Our divergences on political and ideological matters are very great, and the situation has therefore become intolerable. A fighter has to relinquish the pretence of being in agreement with his comrades rather than be at odds with his own conscience, even though, as in my own case, he has no personal blame to lay at their door.

In a study called 'Internal and Dialectical Struggle', published in the *Tribune of Debates*, I have made it sufficiently clear that there need be no personal animus in this kind of internal struggle.

No one can, by speaking either in the name of the workers as a whole, or by any special gift of his own, determine the course of history.

What makes the work of the Executive Committee ineffectual is its lack of mobility, its incapacity to lead the party effectively and directly inside the big industrial firms in the country; also its lack of contact with the peasants. All its activities consist in organizing meetings, and publishing policies and information. No action is planned; the struggle has been abandoned. And in moments of crisis, the party has no grasp on reality, and is unable to make the voices of its leaders heard – as was most evident when Quadros resigned, and when Goulart was deposed. In resigning from the Executive Committee, I wish to state publicly my will to fight, as a revolutionary, alongside the masses; and in doing so, I want also to express my disgust with the political, bureaucratic and conventional play-acting that is going on among the leadership.

One of the points upon which the Executive Committee shows itself especially backward and conservative is the publication of books and the spreading of ideas. Almost a year and a half ago, I published a pamphlet called 'Why I Resisted Imprisonment'. In the past, the leadership would use subterfuges, would confiscate or censor manuscripts; now the comrades of the Executive Committee take note of writings once they have been published, but they never discuss them, even when activists and other leaders demand discussion. That is what happened to my book. Only a year later did they recognize their omission, and pronounce an opinion. They approved the first section, in which I describe my arrest and my time in prison, but disapproved the second, which deals with ideological and political matters in a way they thought contrary to the party line.

It may seem odd that they condemned only one section of a book which forms an obvious unity, for the whole point is the relationship of cause and effect between the two sections. I would never have resisted arrest had I not had political reasons for doing so. Yet the comrades in the leadership passed over this, and took refuge in the abstractions of Kantian agnosticism, which enabled them to separate the inseparable. Furthermore, they declared that no member of the leadership must express his disagreement publicly. That is a Stalinist thesis, which I utterly refute.

A disagreement never appears out of the blue; it is the result of deepening contradictions in the course of a movement's development, and would be much eased by discussion within the movement; in our case such discussion has been non-existent for six years – and the comrades are bent on making it quite impossible! They fall back on that 'theory of unanimity' which has already done us so much harm in the past, and which leads on to the utterly un-Marxist and un-dialectical notion of a monolithic 'kernel of leadership', cut off from the base. They are trying to intimidate us ideologically, and prevent us by force from circulating the ideas they are afraid of. Yet by merely revealing the contradictions that exist, we are on the way to resolving them, if only because in confronting them we also use a practical course as our criterion of truth.

Our disharmony is not of recent date; it goes back to the resignation of Jânio Quadros, when it became clear that we were neither politically nor ideologically equipped to cope with the situation.

In 1962, I presented the Party Assembly with a criticism of our non-Marxist methods, the traces of individualism remaining even in the heart of the leadership, and our failure to commit ourselves ideologically. The coup of April 1964, which met no resistance whatever, proved once again that we were not equal to our mission, and it was at that point that I determined that I, personally, would resist the dictatorship's police.

Today a great many activists are questioning the Party line. It is indeed the sheerest historic fatalism to declare that the bourgeoisie is the moving spirit of the Brazilian revolution, and that the proletariat's action must be subordinate to it – denying the people all initiative, and making them the plaything of events.

The articles I brought together and published under the title *The Brazilian Crisis* were intended precisely to contribute to this debate on the positions taken up by the leadership, positions which I have contested publicly, in the name of free discussion. There is nothing wrong in attacking the executive, for what everyone wants is for it to move into action, and return to dialectical materialism.

The Executive Committee comforts itself with illusions. A good number of its members – if they will forgive my saying so – believed in such middle-class leaders as Kubitschek, Jânio Quadros, Adhemar de Barros,* Generals Amauri Kruel and

* Former governor of Sâo Paulo State.

Justino Alves, and others, and had faith in their promises to resist the dictatorship. Even the suppression of Adhemar de Barros's political rights failed to enlighten them, for the executive then uncritically declared itself in favour of the 'Broad Front',* without giving the masses any notion of what it might mean. In fact, the fascist leader Lacerda intended to use it as a means to founding his own party which he wanted to present as a reformist and popular one. The executive saw this as 'a positive political action' (see *The Workers' Voice*, No. 22, November 1966) and felt that the Front would be able to fight against the dictatorship in favour of the true interests and liberties of the people of Brazil.

What Lacerda actually wanted was to assist American imperialism in a different way, and prevent the liberation of our people. For class reasons, Lacerda would have been incapable of combating the *latifúndio* and working to help peasants and workers. What he wanted to see was a collaboration among the classes, a conciliation that would play into the hands of President Costa e Silva. The executive remained silent in relation to all of this, nourishing their illusions in terms of a so-called 'broader policy', of the fight against sectarianism and the extreme Left, and with contempt for the ideology of the proletariat. They abandoned part of their Marxism, just as they abandoned their independence of class, to become lackeys of the bourgeoisie – whereas the role of the executive should have been to denounce to the people those responsible for the coup and their crimes, and to attack them in true proletarian – or, as Marx would say, 'plebeian' – fashion.

The executive still hopes to inflict upon the dictatorship 'electoral losses that will weaken it', and attributes tremendous importance to the Brazilian Democratic Movement† which it believes capable of drawing to itself the major forces hostile to the régime. It wants to overthrow the dictatorship gently,

* That 'broad front' founded by Lacerda, Kubitschek and Goulart was directed to defend the return of civilians to power, and to achieving a policy of 're-democratization'.

† The one opposition party tolerated by the dictatorship.

without actually attacking the dictators, by uniting Greeks with Trojans! Instead of working out revolutionary tactics and strategy, it is hoping for an illusory re-democratization, through a peaceful solution that is just not possible. These men would seem simply not to have understood Lenin's statement in *The Two Tactics* that 'the great problems of people's lives are only resolved by force' and that victory 'can only be guaranteed by the armed force of the masses, can only depend on insurrection – not on this or that legal and peaceful institution'.

Having said over and over again that the violence of the ruling classes must be opposed by that of the masses, nothing has been done to put the words into action. They go on preaching pacifism, for they lack the revolutionary impetus and awareness that can only arise out of the struggle. For Brazil there is only one possible solution: armed struggle. We have to prepare for an armed rising by the people, with all that that implies. In the past we have said: 'Our influence on the proletariat is as yet wholly insufficient: our influence on the mass of the peasants is minimal; there is still enormous geographical dispersal, underdevelopment, and ignorance among the urban and the rural proletariat.' What we must say now is that 'the revolution will hasten to bring together and inform its scattered forces', that 'every step forward awakens the masses further, and that the programme of revolution draws them irresistibly on, for it alone expresses their true interests, their vital interests'. For there are, in Brazil, revolutionary forces capable of struggling and of resisting the dictatorship. Leninist thinking is shown wherever the proletariat makes its influence felt.

The Executive Committee believes in the leadership of the bourgeoisie; hence arise all our differences of opinion on the problem of the moment, chief among them the problem of the seizure of power. Revolutionaries see this as something that can be achieved only with the participation of the masses. Thus it is not a question of struggling to keep power in the hands of the bourgeoisie, to get a bourgeois government into office – which is what the notion of a nationalist democratic government in fact amounts to. They propose the hypothesis of a 'more or less advanced government' – but this is a euphemism that conceals the fact that a government under the hegemony of the bourgeoisie cannot solve the problems of the people. All this is simply a refusal to engage in revolutionary activity; it is electoralist pacifism and capitulation. The fascist and authoritarian constitution established by the dictatorship, which destroys all State monopoly and defends a reactionary agrarian system, simply hands our country to the United States on a plate, and makes the legislative and judiciary powers mere tools of the executive power, thus making the formation of a democratic government by electoral means quite impossible. If there were such a government, it would inevitably abrogate that constitution, overthrow the dictatorship, and work out quite a different economic system. Short of that, all we can do is spend the next ten or twenty years making electoral compromises which will help the ruling classes and American imperialism to maintain an institutionalized dictatorship in Brazil to assist in repressing any movement of liberation anywhere in Latin America. Compromises of that sort have already discredited us almost wholly in the eyes of the mass of citizens; the time for democratic and liberal revolutions has passed.

Alarmed by the Cuban revolution, North American imperialism – assisted here by the conventional armies of Latin America – does not hesitate to inspire military coups the moment there appears the slightest indication of real liberation in our continent. Nor does it hesitate, if need be, to use the most brutal aggression – as in the case of Vietnam. To talk of a peaceful struggle for basic reforms is a contradiction in terms: such reforms will only come about through revolution, and a change in the military structure and its alliance with the ruling classes. To abandon that is to turn the Marxist party into no more than an appendage of the bourgeois parties.

Furthermore, this subordination to the middle class means a depreciation of the part played by the peasants in the revolution. That is why any political work in the countryside has always met with indifference if not positive ill-will from the Executive Committee. Yet the peasant is a decisive factor in the revolutionary balance: if the peasants do not join them, the proletariat will continue to gravitate round the middle class. In Brazil Marxism is being flagrantly flouted in this manner: by marginalizing the peasants, it is easier to make political and electoral compromises, and indeed out-and-out bargains, with the middle class.

All these reasons compel me to present my resignation; I may add that it is quite impossible for me to accept any form of ideological compromise.

The Executive Committee seems to me to undervalue the role the Party can play in big business, and therefore is not fulfilling it. One can, after all, hardly talk of revolution without basing oneself on the working class, especially in São Paulo where we have the largest and most influential concentration of workers in the country. Yet in São Paulo, because the Party has no strength in the factories, it is in the disastrous situation of being totally subject to the ideological influences of the middle class. The Executive Committee is, apparently, quite indifferent to this state of things. And when the militants of that state's Party elected to their leadership a member of the Executive Committee* and another national leader, that same committee opposed it. They invoked an article from a non-existent resolution stipulating that members of the Executive Committee could not belong to the leadership of any state Party – which would indeed place them in an ivory tower! Extremely dissatisfied, the São Paulo members removed from the leadership all the members appointed by the national Party executive – who had in any case disappointed them by their openness to the bourgeois ideology defended by President Jânio Quadros and Governor Adhemar de Barros. In São Paulo, that ideology was given as a justification for the so-called policy 'of winning local power' by a Party which decided to stop using its proper name, and describe itself as a 'communist movement' within which there could be no room for 'men whose revolt has unbalanced them and made them incapable of correct behaviour on the social level'.

* Marighela himself.

One of the objectives of that 'movement' was a 'democratic restructuring of the administrative machine, the power of the judiciary, and the police system' – a travesty of what the Party should stand for: all these opportunist theses were rejected *en bloc* by the conference assembled in the state of São Paulo. The national Executive Committee responded by going over the heads of the local leadership and intervening directly among our rank and file; and only now, a year afterwards, having destroyed the Party and pushed their acceptance of the bourgeois ideology to its utmost, has the executive at last agreed to discuss the problem of São Paulo. Well: it is for them to try to explain the defection of the intellectuals, the disappearance of the Party from the factories, the failure to do any work among the peasants or to support the revolutionary students. Perhaps they can also explain why some of them are so anxious for electoral compromise! To me the explanation seems to lie in the theoretical and ideological poverty of that executive who were, furthermore, so little on their guard as to let fall into the hands of the police certain documents which gave them the names of people they wanted, and also informed them of some of our internal problems . . .

The Executive Committee cares little for Marxism-Leninism, is not working to produce any developments in theory, refuses to take part in any revolutionary action, fears the publication of books or spreading of the ideas they defend, steers clear of basic problems, preferring a policy of conciliation and an attitude of paternalism.

It is hateful to me to have to say these things, but it is not in my nature to conceal what I really think, either from the Party or from public opinion. I do not believe that individualism or personal action can resolve all these problems. It will be ideas that play the determining role; it will be they that find the echo they need. The Brazilian revolutionary cause, the liberation of our people from the domination of the United States, the unity of the Party in support of Marxist notions – these are the things chiefly at stake. People have a right to expect of us as Communists and Marxist-Leninist revolutionaries that we have the courage to say what we wish and believe, and also the courage to act upon it.

Proletarian greetings,

CARLOS MARIGHELA
Rio de Janeiro, 10 December 1966